The Colors of My Youth

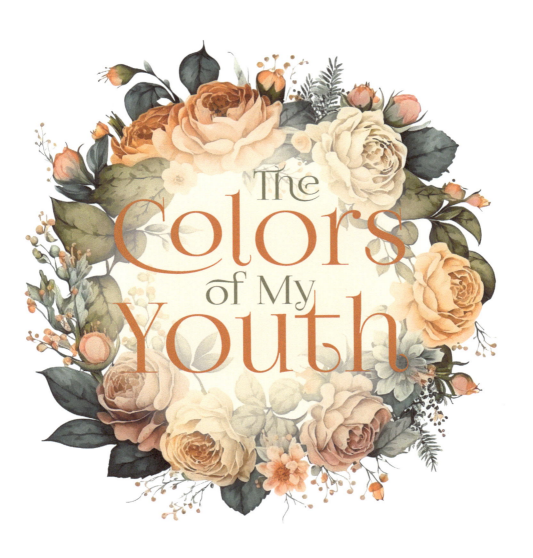

The Colors of My Youth

Jacqueline Johnson Goon

The Colors of My Youth

Copyright © 2024 by Jacqueline Johnson Goon. All rights reserved.

Cover illustration courtesy of Instant Clip Art Oasis © 2024.

No part of this publication may be reproduced, stored in a retrieval system or transmitted in any way by any means, electronic, mechanical, photocopy, recording or otherwise without the prior permission of the author except as provided by USA copyright law.

The opinions expressed by the author are not necessarily those of URLink Print and Media.

1603 Capitol Ave., Suite 310 Cheyenne, Wyoming USA 82001
1-888-980-6523 | admin@urlinkpublishing.com

URLink Print and Media is committed to excellence in the publishing industry.

Book design copyright © 2024 by URLink Print and Media. All rights reserved.

Published in the United States of America

Library of Congress Control Number: 2024921658
ISBN 978-1-68486-956-5 (Paperback)
ISBN 978-1-68486-959-6 (Digital)

02.10.24

REMEMBER

by Christina Georgina Rossetti

Remember me when I am gone away,
Gone far away into the silent land;
When you can no more hold me by the hand,
Nor I half turn to go, yet turning stay.
Remember me when no more, day by day,
You tell me of our future that you planned;
Only remember me; you understand
It will be late to counsel then or pray.
Yet if you should forget me for a while
And afterwards remember, do not grieve;
For if the darkness and corruption leave
A vestige of the thoughts that once I had,
Better by far you should forget and smile
Than that you should remember and be sad.

Acknowledgements

- To my family and friends. Thank you for a lifetime of memories filled with love and laughter. I'm so glad to have walked this journey of life with you.

- To the faculty and staff of McLaurin Elementary Junior High School, 1961-1969. Thank you for lighting the spark and encouraging me to aim for the stars!

Introduction

Looking back at my life, there were times that were frozen in my mind—events and faces of a lifetime ago, each perfect memory seemingly engraved in my heart, pieces of the past and the faces of those I have known who had since elapsed in time.

Not every experience was immortalized, never to be forgotten. But some, which I knew when they were first lived, would remain with me always. Even now, the memories were replayed over and over in my mind where they were destined to live forever.

These memories altogether paint a picture of my soul. A myriad of brilliant colors that form a rainbow within my heart. They were an intricate part of who I was and were as vital as the air I breathe. The hues painted upon the blank canvas of my heart, each vibrant color and experience filled with morals, values, and faith—the foundation of the woman I would become.

These were the colors of my youth.

Prologue

August 1965

It was still dark outside when Mama swept down the small hallway, her black Daniel Green slippers clip-clopping loudly on the cool linoleum floor. Her usual upsy-daisy greeting was met with less cheerful groans as I awoke to a new day.

"Oh, good. You're up." She smiled brightly from the opened doorway. Mom's smile was the last thing I saw at night and the first thing that greeted me each morning. Her warm, caring eyes discreetly scanned the room to see if a pile of soiled linens were on the floor. "You had a good night," she whispered thankfully.

"Yes, Mama," I answered feeling ashamed and proud at the same time. *No spooky soldier ghost standing over me last night. And not too much water before bedtime...this time.* "I had a good night."

Mama looked at me knowingly and turned the white knob on my favorite baby-blue clock radio until soft music began to play. She busied herself tidying the bed covers that were still warm from where I had just been laying.

"Your brother will be up soon," she warned and placed clean undies into my hands. "If you miss the first turn in the bathroom, you'll have to share with dad who's waiting to shave."

Not wasting any more time, I then rushed to the small bathroom too small to comfortably accommodate more than one person at a time. I'd barely finished brushing my teeth before my brother, Mike, was banging on the door for me to get out of there because he had to go.

The image in the mirror of toothpaste foam dripping down my face and chin gave the appearance of a white beard. I wondered how it would be to have long, manicured nails like Mom's. Mike continued to bang on the door. "I'm not done yet," I shouted. Dipping my fingers in warm water, I held them upside down and watched the water trickle in droplets off my fingertips. Smiling, I began to fill the tub with water for my bath.

Sometime later, the banging stopped. I toweled myself dry and opened the door slowly in case Mike was planning to slug me for taking so long. He waited as patiently as he could with his legs and arms crossed tightly as he glared daggers at me from his bedroom door.

"All done," I announced sweetly, knowing I had thrown the first punch this day. He didn't move immediately but just stared at me with eyes squinted tightly and nearly crossed with pain.

Like a cowboy with guns loaded and waiting to draw, I just stood there, blocking his entrance to the coveted room while waiting and watching for him to budge. Without saying a word, I knew he would make me pay big time for putting him through his misery.

"Move! Move!" he finally screamed, rushing past and roughly shoving me aside before slamming the bathroom door in my grinning face.

"Mom-om, Mike pushed me," I cried, rubbing my arm and attempting all I could to create just one tear hoping to get my big brother in trouble again. It didn't matter that I provoked him half of the time.

"I've asked you to stop messing with your brother," Mama's harsh words admonished me, echoing loudly throughout the house. "You're going to be late on the first day of school if you keep poking along." A small snicker behind the bathroom door let me know Mike had heard Mama too.

Clutching my dirty clothes to my chest, I turned and slammed directly into my dad who firmly pushed me aside with one hand and balanced a cup of steaming coffee with the other. "Sorry, Papa," I apologized and scooted into the safety of my room before he could scold me for not looking where I was going and picking fights with my brother.

Mama laid out on the bed the clothes I was to wear to school that day. "Come on, let's get you lotioned up," she said in that voice somewhere between laughing and singing. Mama enjoyed slathering me from head to toe in Jergens lotion, pleased to be sure I had no ashy knees or elbows when she was done.

"Let me check your sores," she said worriedly and applied the sticky ointment the doctor had prescribed. Both of my legs had large open sores caused by a skin rash the doctors said would heal in time. The bleeding ones were caused by me scratching them when I was asleep. Mama covered those with a bandage and warned me not to scratch the smaller ones that were almost healed.

She finished administering care to my sores and helped me don knee-high socks to also cover them. I secured the straps of my favorite Mary Jane shoes Papa had polished the night before. "Keep your socks pulled up," Mama reminded me, "so the other kids won't make fun of you like in kindergarten. Okay, baby?"

I didn't need Mama to remind me of how cruel my friends and teachers had been. As an adult, she understood the concerns other parents and the teachers had and their precaution to ensure what affected her child was not contagious. But as a child, the forced separation and teasing was both hurtful and humiliating.

The last day at Mama Jordan's Daycare was the most painful experience. Deciding to treat the students to a day at the swimming pool at Jackson State's College Park, Mama had dressed me in a swimsuit only to hear the pool attendants would not allow me to put even a toe in the cool water.

The whole day I had to sit far enough back from the pool they felt would not contaminate the water while the entire class played and swam and splashed water onto me and my infected legs. "Okay, Mama," I said thoughtfully, wondering if I would ever outlive the embarrassment.

Ten minutes later, I was dressed in a pretty blue-and-green plaid dress with a white scalloped collar with blue piping. Mike was dressed also, and I joined him for breakfast. The dining table was set with all the foods Mama had prepared earlier—large bowlfuls of creamy oatmeal with offerings of butter, preserves, honey and syrup, creamy hominy grits, scrambled eggs, bacon, sausage patties, and buttered toast and milk.

"Eat up," Mama said and pulled a bar stool up behind my chair. While I ate, she oiled my hair, brushing it neatly into two ponytails. "The bus will be here soon," she told us again to eat faster and tied blue-and-green ribbons in my hair.

Gathering our book satchels filled with new pencils, composition tablets, and lunch money for the week, Mike and I stood on the front stoop, waiting to walk the long driveway to Monterey Road until our older cousins could be seen walking down our grandparents' driveway next door where the Route 21 school bus for Rankin County would stop first to pick them up.

Kids were crammed into the large yellow bus like sardines in a metal tin can. It was one big noisy joyride of friends and relatives alike. Everyone's excited about the first day of school and what their new teachers would be like. Getting a seat depended on the route the driver chose to drive first. We were near the end of the pickup route, so standing the entire thirty-minute drive to and from school was not uncommon. Those sitting nearest the small aisleway, sometimes offered half of their seats to standers. Those who were seated who didn't particularly care would stare out of the window, at their laps or the backs of someone else's head.

So many of my family lived along Monterey Road, and the bus stopped at every drive picking up so many of us that we could have formed an entire football team. With each stop, the noise level on the bus would increase to an even higher crescendo.

Suddenly the driver slammed on the brakes yelling for everyone to stop talking so he could think. Those of us standing in the aisleway shot forward first two steps and then backward again while gripping our satchels tightly with one hand and slapping blindly at the backs of seats or people to keep from falling.

All eyes were focused on the driver's rearview mirror that showed him eyeballing us back with a stern expression on his face that told everyone he meant business. Without another sound, the bus weaved and swayed its way along the gravel road, barely slowing for oncoming traffic or hapless animals.

Stopping at an intersection, the bus turned right rather than keeping straight on the road, not far from the Berry-Easterling's, my Mama's family farm. Each time the bus was at that intersection of the road I thought lovingly of my granddaddy RT and Grandma Jessie and wondered if they were busily feeding the livestock, milking the cows, or gathering eggs from the henhouse. That thought was soon replaced when the bus slowed again to turn down a long driveway leading to McLaurin School.

Built in 1958, the U-shaped school built primarily for Negro students in the Rankin County school district was the newer educational home for the country school that generations of students and their parents had attended. Surrounded by acres of lush green grass and pine trees, the one-level brick building appeared magnificent as it glowed in the early morning sunlight. A place where, by Johnson or Easterling kin, I was related someway to the principal, several teachers and many students.

Passing two duplex-style homes on the left where the principal and assistant principal resided with their families, the bus drove parallel to a small baseball field before veering left to stop at the entrance doors. Everyone stood at once, anxious to depart the stuffy environment. At the top of narrow steps, two doors opened to welcome the students to a new day.

A long glass cabinet was placed against a wall to the left just inside the entrance doors. The locked case proudly displayed numerous awards and trophies shaped on top with gold basketballs, baseballs, or footballs were inscribed with the names and dates of tournaments that both male and female teams had won or placed second or third in. Ribbons, certificates, and newspaper articles depicting the triumphant performances were also framed and included in the athletic monument.

To the right was the entrance to the cafeteria, and just beyond a large green-and-gold banner bearing a Tiger, the school's mascot, hung with distinction in a small hallway leading to the stage and auditorium that also served as the basketball court. The elementary wing lay straight ahead from the display case, while to the left was the school office and junior high and high school wings that lay beyond. Everyone hurried to reach their new classroom assignments before they would be marked tardy and require an excuse from the administration office before they could re-enter the classroom.

Buildings housing the kitchens, cafeteria, mechanics shop, and band room were situated beyond leading back toward a football field and bleachers on one side of the field where McLaurin students and alumni could sit while cheering the home team. Sadly, fans of the visiting teams had to stand on the opposite side of the field.

The land slopped upward from the football field toward the elementary wing of the school, and just beyond was a playground of a small and large set of swings and slides or open land for playing tag, softball, hide-and-seek, dodge ball, or just to sit quietly and read. Teachers with classes in recess huddled together where they sat in strategic locations to oversee the entire play areas.

Breathing deeply, the mingled smells of books and pine cleaner used to mop the tile floors were both welcoming and terrifying. Already the cooks were busily preparing the school luncheon, and the aromas of hamburgers and fries wafted beyond the closed cafeteria doors to make my stomach rumble loudly.

Mike stopped only long enough to ask if I had my lunch money and told me to hurry along to Mrs. King's classroom before I was marked late. Before I could speak to him, he had turned and was hurrying down the junior high wing toward his own classroom when a warning bell rang loudly.

Mrs. King's sixth grade classroom was at the end of the long hallway. I hurried inside just as the school's second bell rang for classes to begin. The classroom was filled with students I had known since first grade, and it was good to see everyone smiling and happy to be together again.

The teacher had a sitting chart prepared and rearranged everyone in alphabetical order. Before long, the attendance roll had been called and we were issued the books we'd need for the year.

The first homework assignment was to write an essay about what we did during the summer vacation. Mrs. King said the paper should be at least five pages in length, and she warned us that she would be grading us on our penmanship and grammar. She designated the last two hours of school for us to begin our essays.

So much had happened during my vacation that I didn't know what specifically I should write about. Unsure how to begin, I tentatively raised my hand and waited. Before long, Mrs. King was standing at my desk and wanted to know how she could help me.

"I don't know how to begin," I said timidly. "What I mean is, I don't know which thing to write about," I quickly added, not wanting her to think I would fail the assignment.

"Why don't you try writing a little about everything," she whispered and smiled. Turning to address the entire class, she continued speaking. "Everyone, think about your experiences first, and jot down your thoughts." She added, "That should make it easier for the words to flow."

"Does that help?" she asked expectantly and returned to her desk without waiting for me to reply.

I chewed my bottom lip in my nervous habit and picked up my pencil to begin. Nothing. I got up to sharpen my pencil and saw all of my classmates busily writing about their summer adventures. I returned to my seat and began to write. "This summer I..." And once again my mind was blank.

I looked up to see Mrs. King watching me anxiously and smiled. "Everything okay?" she asked and seemed to believe me when I said it was. Her family lived across the street from ours in Jackson before Mama and Daddy built our home in the country. Her stern look let me know she was my teacher then and had different expectations of me than as my former neighbor and babysitter.

Think about your experiences first, and jot down your thoughts. I wrote down just the things I had done, and before long, the words began to flow in my mind. What Mrs. King had suggested worked! But now I had a much bigger problem. I shook my head sadly wondering how in the world was I supposed to condense three months of summer onto five pages of wide-ruled paper.

Chapter One

Gold
Happiness, Comfort

It was one of those typical hot summer days in Mississippi—full of heat, humidity, and killer mosquitoes. I hurriedly dressed, anxious to be outside where, for a child, the day beckoned of unexplored adventures, mischief, and mayhem.

My mom, dad, brother, and I lived in the house that dad had built nine years earlier. My bedroom was near the front of the house, but my favorite place had always been looking out the window of my brother's room, which gave a peaceful view of blue hydrangea shrubs, vegetable gardens, and pasture leading toward our grandparents' home located five hundred yards away.

The large country home was painted white with eight steps leading to the front porch, which had two pillars supporting the roof overhang. My brother, Mike, and I were often teased about how in the first years after our move to Florence we'd sat quietly together there watching the road for our parents to return home from the city of Jackson where they worked about thirty miles north of Florence.

This was my second favorite spot to be, just sitting and watching the clouds and cars go by, surrounded by the sweet smells of my grandma Ada's cherished flowers—azaleas, sweet lavender, Christmas cactus, honeysuckle, and one she'd called four o'clocks, because that's the time we watched them open each day. Grandma Ada reminded me in many ways of her flower garden in that she was small and fragile yet strong and resilient, beautiful and sweet.

Anxious to get outside, I entered Mike's room as usual without knocking. He was already dressed in a baseball jersey and jeans. He sat on the edge of the bed and propped his foot while beginning to lace his favorite pair of Converse sneakers. I attempted to position myself next to him as always. It wasn't long that he was shouting for me to get off the bed he'd just made.

It hadn't been that long ago that I'd been made to vacate the bottom bunk bed in Mike's room for my own. For years, we'd shared a room until mom decided Mike should have the privacy of his own room, probably to Mike's great relief. To help convince me of this, Dad spent a great deal of time converting my room at the front of the house into a little girl's dream.

I guess other girls would've been tickled to have a room like mine—filled with pink walls, ruffled bed skirts, baby dolls, and doll houses. Not me, though. I loved everything about my brother's bedroom. He had bats and balls, trains, race cars, and, best of all, my favorite window!

Nearly done lacing his shoes now, Mike glanced up to see me staring at the cars beginning to crowd the driveway next door. There was a feeling of anticipation in the air when I turned to see him looking too because like me, he knew the cars had brought cousins that would help make up the teams for the ongoing baseball challenge of boys versus girls. This was the day the boys had declared would show they were mightier than a bunch of sissy girls, and it was the day the girls felt would show they could play better than the boys, if not as well as.

The day was the same as all Sundays when aunts, uncles, and cousins would come to visit. Dinner was served potluck style where every room in the house was filled with laughter and merriment. On bright sunny days like today, picnic tables were erected outside where dinner would be served buffet style. The lawn would be covered with relatives, all eating, drinking, and enjoying the peaceful contentment of being home with family.

The same as every other Sunday, following dinner, the women sat huddled in the cool shade beneath a chinaberry tree on the front lawn, catching up on the latest family news, the latest gossip, or soap opera cliffhangers. The men positioned themselves nearby, propping themselves on trees, stumps, or cars doing the same but swearing differently. Everyone stopped to wave at neighbors who shouted out or tooted their car horns while zooming past on the road below.

The boys were busy recreating the baseball field used for decades between two large elm trees. Hal was the oldest and played on the high school team, so he was generally in charge of measurements between bases; Larry and Jerry (who was nicknamed, Bo) were busy getting the two bats and one ball; and Jimmy set up the pitcher's mound while Mike placed old rags or cardboard on the spots Hal had marked for bases. The girls were busy enough deciding what positions to play.

An ice cream machine hummed nearby on the back porch where Aunt Beatrice, who was assigned to that particular duty for the day, continued to oversee the level of ice and salt needed to chill the metal bucket as it churned the delicious custard treat. Before leaving to get more ice from the kitchen freezer, she issued an order that we'd better be careful.

The battered balls and bats were examined and judged useable once again. Normally the games were played with a standard softball, except it had been split open during the last game when Larry had hit a home run. Hal offered instead a smaller and harder baseball for us to use. With the field ready, a coin was tossed to see who would take the field first. Girls called for heads; it was tails. We each picked up a glove from the stack at home plate.

The girls all showed some trepidation about using a smaller, much harder ball. The boys seemed willing, so there probably wasn't anything to worry about. Taking my position in the outfield, I decided it wouldn't matter much anyway because I'd just let the ball hit the ground before picking it up and thus spare my palms any injury.

My twin cousins, Brenda and Linda, both assumed the role of team captain mainly because they were equally respected. Brenda assumed the position at first base; Linda, third; Sandra, second; and Lawanda, pitcher. I wanted to be pitcher at every game, but being the smallest, I was always told it would be better for me to play outfield to avoid getting hurt.

I suppose my clothing had something to do with my relegation to the outfield too. You see, my mom had always sewn a closet full of playsets for me to wear during the summer. This particular day, I'd made the wrong choice of wearing a beautiful white short set, very cute with colorful small flowers and eyelet lace trim but very inappropriate in a must-win, do-or-die baseball game. Oh well, I sighed, I may be in outfield, but I'm looking good. I flicked at a wasp that buzzed near my head then waited for the first pitch and the ball that would come my way.

Most of the first hits were within the baselines, and the girls made easy outs. It was difficult, however, to score from hits made. After several innings of the same failure, the boys began to boast that they were being gentle at the coaxing of the aunts, uncles, and relatives watching the game. When asked not to do us any favors, they openly declared war and swore to smear our noses in it. I guess we should have taken them seriously.

Toward the bottom of the fifth inning, the score was tied at three to three. Mike was on first, and Larry was on second. Hal was at bat. During most of the game, San and Bren had fallen back from their positions to play mine too. It was bad enough that I couldn't even get to first base to help score points. The anger I'd had at being dismissed to outfield was passing; I wanted to show I could be a part of the team too.

I was daydreaming from my spot in outfield when Hal hit the ball right toward me. Bren and San were already abandoning their positions to fall back toward mine while Wanda was running to cover home plate, and Lin was attempting to block Larry's run to third.

I flexed Mike's prized left-hander's glove in my right hand and ran backward, wondering how I was going to throw the caught ball with my left hand anyway.

Nevertheless, my eyes remained steady on the ball coming closer and closer toward me. This was my chance to prove I was just as good a baseball player as everyone else. The ball was starting to descend now. Lifting my hand, I opened the glove to reveal the pouch Mike had said the ball should drop into; otherwise, I would feel a sting where the ball might hit the palm of my hand if not the top of my head.

Like a rewinding tape, over and over I thought, *I can do this. I can do this.* A few more steps and I'd have it! Twice I shout that, "I've got it!" Suddenly, the ground below me vanished. Someone shouted for me to look out before the ball, Mike's prized glove, and I began spiraling down a fifty feet embankment.

I'd fallen to the bottom of the gravel road beneath. Miraculously, I had landed gently at the rocky edge and was uninjured. I looked up to see Bren peering down at me from the embankment and asking if I was okay. There was laughter and concern in her voice. I guess it was pretty comical seeing me sprawled at the bottom of the road, on my back with my legs dangling in the bushes.

I answer feebly that I'm okay then hurry to grab the baseball in the ditch across the road. I toss the ball up to Bren who attempts to help me up the embankment. In the end, I had to walk the long driveway back to my position in the outfield. After everyone was assured I was uninjured, there was much laughter, taunts, and teasing. I was more embarrassed that my beautiful white short set with the small colorful flowers and eyelet lace trim was completely covered with dirt, leaves, and twigs. My face, arms, and legs were covered with dirt and grime. My hair was a mess with pieces of twig intermixed. My team called for time-out, and I ran home to check for scratches and clean myself up a bit. Baseball was becoming a dirty sport indeed.

The top of the seventh inning, the boys were ahead by three. Even so, the girls remained confident that we could still win the game. Probably to intimidate the boys some, Wanda had begun to inch forward from the pitcher's mound despite warnings she'd been receiving to step back or suffer!

I suppose that was a challenge in itself because the more they advised her to take some steps backward, the more she persisted to inch her way forward. From the outfield, I was still smarting from not being given the chance to pitch, not having gotten to first base, ruining my beautiful white short set with the small colorful flowers and eyelet lace trim, and my infamous express flight to the road below!

From my position in the outfield, I tried to hear the arguments going on between the pitcher's mound and home plate. Wanda and I found something to fight about nearly every day. I knew what it was like to argue a losing cause with her. I shielded my eyes from the hot sun, swatted at a mosquito on my leg, and prepared myself for a long wait.

There was concern that Wanda may get hurt if she didn't take everybody's advice and move back the way someone with common sense would. I was beginning to itch from head to toe and wanted to go home to shower and change. Some people just won't listen, though. With growing frustration, I decided if Wanda insisted on living dangerously, then so be it. Not long after that thought, Larry came up to bat. He asked her again to step back behind the pitcher's mound. She refused.

Have you ever seen some things happen, and as you recall them time after time, it all seems to replay in slow motion in your mind? Well, that's the way everyone there recalled what happened next.

I suppose Wanda's choice to stand her ground would have been a noble cause had she really had something to be noble about. In this case, she was just plain stubborn. After the final warning, Larry pointed his finger directly at her smirking face and foretold that the ball was being sent directly there.

With an extra step forward, Wanda released the ball to home plate. And then comes that moment when time freezes and you can only watch in horrow knowing something really bad is about to happen but you can neither stop it nor look away. No sooner had the ball left her hand when a crack of the bat slammed it soundly between her two front teeth with exact radar precision. With her backward fall, all the aunts, uncles, and relatives came running, the two rival teams circled the fallen, foolish hero.

Her mom, Aunt Helen, fetched ice from the humming metal bucket, and a towel was pulled from the clothes-line filled with ice and placed at poor naïve Wanda's bleeding mouth. A chipped tooth was all she'd suffered, but I suppose no one had to tell her she was lucky she didn't lose a whole head of teeth that day.

And with that, the game was over, and no one cared that the boys had won or the girls had lost. The challenge of the day was repeated in countless games of baseball, basketball, football, and volleyball.

Sometimes the boys and girls played against each other. Most times, though, we united to challenge other families up and down Monterey Road. The grueling games often resulted in bruised limbs or occasional broken bones. I often have fond memories of those days.

It was a time when the simple pleasures of family dinners, backyard reunions, and homemade ice cream were taken for granted, the memories to be cherished despite the years and distance that now separates us.

Gone was the time of our childhood, full of great adventures and life's challenges, not to see how much better or stronger or different we may be from one another but rather to discover how very much alike we were, especially when there was love in our hearts.

Chapter Two

Purple
Wisdom, Thoughtfulness

If you'd ask any city kid what they'd consider the best way to spend Saturdays, chances are it'd be a day in the park, swimming, hiking, or shopping. Growing up in Florence, Mississippi, when asked the same thing, I always, always said the best way to spend Saturdays was a trip to Jackson. Located thirty miles north of Florence, Jackson was a mecca of specialty and clothing shops, fine restaurants, museums, and tall buildings, which attributed to the charm of this growing metropolitan city.

For years, the drive to Jackson every Saturday never changed. I'd dress with care, rushing to join my cousins, Sandra and Lawanda, next door. Daddy Eli always threatened to leave everyone behind if we weren't ready by noon. He never could carry out his threat, however, because we'd always end up waiting for my grandmother, Ada. No matter how much he wanted to, he'd always concede to wait and pout.

He was a thin dark man and stood over six feet tall. Grandma's family was white, and she had blue-gray eyes and long straight hair that looked like spun silver she always painstakingly plaited and then pinned into a bun on the back of her head. My grandmother always seemed to get the best of him. Sometimes he'd become impatient and try to complain. That didn't seem to faze her any, though. Standing shy of five feet tall, she'd pause between finishing her hair or checking the contents of her handbag and sweetly suggest that he hush up and go wait in the car, and that would be the end of that. The response was always the same. Once I caught him smiling and knew he was partly teasing her and partly serious but knew it would do no good to argue. My grandpa was a very wise man.

We'd watch *American Bandstand* while waiting for my grandmother to dress. Sometimes the delivery truck for Borden milk products would come by, and on really hot days, one of us would wait at the road to flag him down so we could spend whatever change we had on Popsicles and other ice cream treats.

When it was time to go, San, Wanda, and I would take our usual places on the back seat of my granddaddy's old Chevrolet. I always ended up in the middle, probably because I was the smallest. Hoping to get another word in, Granddad would grump about us taking so long to leave as though he was going to miss an important engagement. In nearly ten years, his agenda rarely changed, though.

Upon arriving downtown, Granddad would usually find a parking spot on Lamar Street near Walgreen's Drugstore or J. C. Penney's. After disembarking the car, we'd stretched our limbs, smoothed any wayward hair, and cursed any wrinkles to our neatly ironed skirts. Without fail, my grandfather would issue a curt order for us to meet back at the car at a chosen time. Most times, we'd separate within seconds. He would head off in an unknown direction leaving my grandmother, cousins, and I to be free to take care of any womanly needs.

Although lighter skinned than a lot of blacks, I didn't inherit my grandmother's coloring as much as my cousins, so I gathered the most looks from whites who stared their displeasure directly at me. Mama Ada never met their stares directly, although I knew she had to be aware of their silent censure. With quiet dignity, she went on about her business, shuffling us safely from store to store.

Self-consciously, I would drag a few steps behind to avoid any additional looks designed to put her or me in our places. I never asked if that was why Grandpa was rarely seen until we'd meet at the designated spot he and Grandma had agreed upon, and it was near time to load up our packages, head to the Jitney Jungle grocery, and return home.

Like baby chicks, we'd trail along beside my grandmother through the crowds walking every direction on Capitol Street. Reigning in our youthful excitement to browse every storefront window, our steps were shifted to a slower pace for Grandma.

My mom and aunts worked at businesses along East Capitol Street near the Governor's Mansion and Old Capitol Museum. Mom worked at Mori's Luggage & Gifts, Aunt Floree at McRae's fine department store, while Aunts Beatrice and Helen worked at a diner that served the best sandwiches and soda fountain drinks. Although Mama Ada rarely permitted us to visit them at work, they always seemed pleased whenever we briefly stopped by.

This Saturday was rainy, the midwinter air sending brisk chills up the tails of our coats. My grandmother secured the fur collar of her tan wool coat to block the cold breeze. Sandra covered her ears with a wool tam and shivered, turning to shield her face from the wind.

I thanked the heavens for the warm boots I wore and tucked my ungloved hands into even colder pockets. However, Wanda seemed the most comfortable of us all.

Sporting a new black coat, she walked with a confidence the rest of us were far from feeling. You know how good it feels when you have on something brand spanking new and how nobody can say you don't look good wearing it? Well, I guess that's how Wanda was that day. Simply stated, she really loved her new black vinyl coat.

We had a routine to follow. Our favorite places to browse were the trendy but economical shops along East Capitol Street. We always had a reason to visit the corner drugstore or J. C. Penney's. Another favorite place for me was the Scottie drugstore. I always like the Scottish tartan print design used in decorations in the store, and the air always smelled sweet and clean inside.

Sometimes, we shopped at Sears off State Street just down from the Old Capitol and War Memorial Museums. I liked going there best of all, mainly because of the wonderful smells coming from the counters where popcorn, candies, and sweet nuts were sold. My pediatrician's office was across from Sears off State Street. I loved going there because he would always give me red lollipops.

That particular Saturday, Sandra needed a slip, so we limited our shopping to J. C. Penney's. I remember browsing through the second floor departments where women's lingerie, clothing, and accessories were sold. Shopping completed, we were leaving to join my grandparents in the appliance department on the bottom level when my boot heel caught in the torn vinyl covering the second stair.

Falling headfirst, I reached out frantically for anything that could save me. Fortunately, Wanda was closest to me. Unfortunately, the only thing I could grab a hold of was the left pocket of her new coat.

Within seconds, I was spiraling downward, my head bumping and rolling over nearly ten steps, my legs and arms a tangled mess, my body becoming bruised and scratched, and in my hand was a black imitation leather coat pocket complete with a six-inch trailer of insulated lining.

I heard several loud screams. The sounds seemed so far away, ghoulish, and somehow inhuman. I wasn't sure if the cries were my own for my pitiful fall or if the cries were Wanda for her more pitiable coat.

I stumbled to my feet with the help of my cousins who lifted me from the stairs cautiously and a bit dazed. My head was spinning making me dizzy and nauseous. I took a few steps through a divider door, which led to the last flight of steps to the bottom level.

While trying to get a sure footing on the first step, my legs collapsed beneath me. I slipped from the hands that were supporting me and began tumbling down the last flight of stairs.

Fifteen steps later, I lay sprawled at the base of the stairway in the men's department. To my left was a display of Hanes underwear, to my right an arrangement of neckties. When I opened my eyes, an employee was leaning over me and asking if I was okay. I weakly replied I was and bypassed his assistance for anything more than to help steer me toward an exit with no stairs where I slowly limped my way out of the store.

Upon leaving, Sandra had to place a restraining hand on my shoulder to prevent me from falling in front of a moving car. I'd suffered and survived two terrible falls and miraculously had no broken neck to show for it.

The final lap of our Saturday ride always ended with grocery shopping at the Jitney-Jungle, a stop at the Hardin's Bread thrift shop, and a quick visit to the pharmacy department at New Deal supermarket on Highway 49.

We always bought treats at each, but there was a shadow of gloom to what had started out a beautiful day. For me, my body throbbed all over. My head felt like I had been hit with a sledgehammer, and I had double vision.

The quiet feeling of gloom, which fell over us was for a much worse tragedy, one we could not begin to understand. I placed the left coat pocket and dangling insulated lining above the ripped opening on Wanda's coat. I remember thinking my mom, who was by all accounts one of the finest seamstresses in Rankin County, couldn't salvage what was left of Wanda's coat.

I smiled wanly and said Mom would be able fix it. The statement was lost as everyone was silently contemplating what to do.

Sandra appeared interested in something outside the window. Mama Ada stared silently ahead while Daddy Eli seemed content to be on his way. I tried looking straight ahead and outside the window, but my eyes kept straying back to the massive gap in Wanda's coat.

She sat beside me, completely silent and still, her mood equal to someone in deep mourning or about to commit murder. Her eyes were filled with unshed tears. I remember wishing I had broken an arm or something to make it all seem worthwhile. I always wondered if Wanda had felt the same too.

By Monday, my bruises had begun to heal, my migraines had decreased to mild headaches, and my eyesight had returned to a normal nearsightedness.

Mom wasn't particularly flattered when I suggested she could fix Wanda's coat since the damage to the vinyl was beyond repair. In the end, Wanda had received the gift of a new coat.

In time, I was forgiven for destroying the other coat but had to endure teasings about not getting too close to the replacement jacket. I don't remember much about Wanda's new coat, but I am sure of two things. One, it was not black, and two, it was made of worsted wool.

Chapter Three

Black
Death, Evil

Growing up in Florence was the best a girl could hope for. In this small rural community located thirty miles south of Jackson, Mississippi, I was afforded the wholesomeness of good country living and the sophistication of city girls when on short trips to the state capital. By all standards, my family was no different from most others in my community, although we were slightly better off than some.

When I was five and my brother a year older, my dad decided to build a home on land adjacent to my grandparents. The city life was not what my father had in mind for my brother and me, so putting all sophisticated ways behind us, we closed the lease on the duplex where we'd lived all my life in Jackson and moved to our new home in Florence.

The paved road off Highway 49 curved through rich countryside where white folks lived in big country homes with wide front porches that invited passersby to rest awhile. Others were not as welcoming, openly displaying Union Jack flags on lawns decorated with black boy hitching posts.

No one seemed to mind black folks just passing by, as long as it was understood that you keep going. I remembered thinking how funny it would be if any of them were also related to me by my Grandma Ada's family, the Hampton's, who were all white and also resided in Florence. I am of the Johnson family, and growing up, I heard jokes that there were so many of us in Florence, they ought to change the name of the town to Johnsonville. I reckon there were quite a lot of us. Heck, rumor was that a distant relative had as many as fifteen kids!

The road we lived off of was about three miles from the main highway, branching off the paved road at a wide curve. Our road was gravel and rock, though. Hearing the sound of gravel crunching underneath car wheels made me feel good inside, I guess because it signaled that company was coming. Most times, I'd say I preferred a graveled road to a paved one—particularly in summertime when it was nearly impossible to walk barefoot to Cousin Elizabeth's country store situated off Monterey Road that was paved.

I used to be envious of my relatives who had land between the white folks in that stretch of town. I remember thinking they'd probably had things a whole lot better than the rest of us. Years later, I'd know it didn't much matter. Not so much because of the equality of our races or where our homes were built, but because the land itself was tainted.

I'm not exactly sure where it begins or ends, but somewhere along that paved road that leads from the main highway, you begin to get the eerie feeling of being watched or followed. It's almost suffocating to the point that the hair stands high on your neck, and your heart beats faster with every minute. There's some areas where you get that spooky feeling from twilight to dawn. Then there's other places inside the unknown radius where the elm, poplar, and pine trees stand tall and mighty, where the sun does not shine nor the wind blows, where time seems to stand still and day or night, you know you're not alone and what's there you don't like.

I grew up in a place where the land was rich in history, bringing to life the stories of folklore and legend. My granddaddy Eli had told us often about the history of the land. The particular stretch of land we lived on was near a trail the Confederate soldiers followed on their way to or from the battle at Vicksburg. Many died along the way.

In the woods across from our home, we'd found an Indian spearhead on what we later realized was probably a holy burial ground. My brother, Mike, and I returned the spearhead, hoping to honor the warrior buried there. We were afraid to venture too close, so we tossed the flint as close as possible to where we'd found it before running away as though the great warrior himself was chasing us.

There were always tales of some kind about ghosts or headless horsemen in our community. I was walking home one day and looked out at my grandfather's pasture to see a man sitting atop a beautiful black stallion. He was a large man and wore a black rain slicker. I thought how unusual to see a man riding a horse like that in my grandfather's pasture when the horse stopped and reared back on its hind legs. From the distance, I could not see clearly above the man's shoulder. I can't say for sure whether he was headless or not, and I didn't waste time trying to find out.

The most terrifying experiences I had growing up in Florence didn't come from outside but within my home. There was a presence there. Not in certain areas but throughout the house. I remember there being an open area to the ceiling in the area where the water heater was placed just off from the bathroom. Chills rolled down my back each time that door was opened. No matter what time of day, to open that door, you'd be fanned with a breeze and you'd feel the presence of something breathing upon you and sucking the breath out of you at the same time.

Fear was the name I gave it, plain and simple. That deep-down emotion that gives you a major case of the hebbie-jeebies when your mind can't understand what your eyes are seeing. It does no good trying to explain it to anyone. Sometimes they believe you. Most times they call you crazy because maybe a part of them is too scared to believe it can be true. I guess some people have to experience things themselves in order to believe they could really happen. Hey, not me. I'm convinced!

Mama and Daddy had been invited to visit friends in the city one Sunday afternoon. Because the next day was a school day, Mike and I chose to stay home to finish our homework and then go to bed early. Around nine o'clock, we heard footsteps walking hard and fast up to the door off from the garage. The garage light was on, and Mike and I stood there listening to footsteps coming toward us, but no one was there. The footsteps stopped at the door, and immediately, we felt a presence in the room with us.

Mike asked me if I had heard what he had heard. I said I had and was frightened even more by the look of fear on my brother's face. He whispered that he was going to turn on the front porch light and asked me to turn on the light for the backyard at the same time. We did each simultaneously and began looking for any sign that someone was there.

Convinced there was no one there but feeling the overwhelming presence of something in the house with us, Mike called our grandfather, Daddy Eli, and told him what had happened and we were scared. Our grandparents never placed a foot in our home after something had chased my Grandma Ada out while she had watched her precious *As the World Turns* soap opera on our new color TV. She never said exactly what happened, only that she'd never cross the threshold again, and she never did.

We pleaded with Daddy Eli to come get us, but with equal fear in his voice, he told us he would turn their front porch light on and when we saw him standing there to run as fast as we can.

Mike scribbled a quick note for our parents then barely gave me time to get beside him before he took off running into the darkness and toward the light so far away. I was one step behind him. We waited there for hours until our parents came and made us reluctantly return home.

Years later, I can laugh at Daddy Eli's brave heroics on our behalf that night. If given the choice, I wouldn't have budged off that lighted porch either. Did I mention my grandfather was over six feet tall with big, strong hands and dark beautiful eyes filled with kindness and knowledge. He was a quiet man who spoke little, but his words were powerful when he spoke. He was known in Rankin County as being a very wise man. In this, we are alike.

My dad worked second shift for the bus transit system in Jackson. His shift ended at midnight, and he usually arrived home around 1:30 a.m. Mom was awakened to the sound of the front door opening and closing then the sound of dragging footsteps. Assuming it was my dad arriving home, she called out to him several times, particularly because she noticed he wasn't turning any lights on. The sound of the dragging footsteps continued past my bedroom down the short hallway to my parents' room.

Mom became frightened at this point and pulled the covers over her head. The footsteps continued up to her bed, but there was no one there. At that moment, my dad arrived home.

I couldn't say exactly when it all began, but it was one of my earliest memories of my childhood. At first I didn't know what to make of the weird experiences, so like all kids, I talked to my friends at school about it. As would be expected, though, no one believed me.

Each night between midnight and dawn, I would awaken to the sounds of the front door opening and closing then the sound of someone dragging their feet across the linoleum. Each night, it was like a ritual. The sounds would continue up to my doorway then stop. At that moment, the side of my bed would dip as though someone had sat on it, and I would feel the slight indentation of my covers from my lowest bottom position to the tip of my head.

If my legs were outstretched, at the side of my foot I would feel a small dip, which would continue up to my head about six or eight inches apart. If I had fallen asleep in a fetal position, the indentations would begin at my hip then continue upward to the tip of my head. I do not remember anything after that.

Some nights I would hear the front door open and would jump from my bed to run down the small hallway to my parent's bedroom. The sound of dragging footsteps followed steadily behind me, all the while the hallway lengthened, and the walls closed in around me like a tunnel, as I ran steadily in a terrifyingly slow motion always into the safety of my mother's arms.

One night I had fallen asleep with my back to the doorway. This particular night, I had not been awakened by the sounds of the door or footsteps. I became fully awake and had the urge to turn over. When I did, I saw the general for the first and only time. He was both frightening and magnificent just standing there watching over me.

Standing beside my bed as though he had come to wish me good night, he was dressed in full Confederate regalia. His double-breasted coat was buttoned with tassels falling across his chest and at each shoulder. A sword and holster with gun hung from his waist. In his hand, he carried a long-barreled rifle. The cap atop his head was set neat and straight, the emblem above the bib that of two crossing rifles. The general had a thick mustache and kind, gentle eyes.

The aura around him was a soft glow. I could see my bedroom furniture behind him, through the hazy color that allowed me to see him as well. I was not afraid but rather pleased he had allowed me to see him also. I simply closed my eyes and went to sleep.

My bedroom furniture had been in the same position for years. The visits from the general were the same, and occasionally, I'd sleep right through them. Not often, though. I decided to rearrange my furniture, placing the side of my bed the general always stood next to only three inches from the side wall, allowing only enough room to tuck the bedspread neatly.

That night, the sound of the door and footsteps began as usual, except this time the sound didn't stop at my door. This frightened me because all the horrible experiences we had faced had been consistent over the years. I didn't know how to interpret this change as I listened to the footsteps continue past the left side of my bed, then the foot of the bed, and to my horror, up the right side of the bed. The footsteps were loud and strong as though there were three feet separating the bed and wall rather than three inches.

Another difference was that I had the covers over my head and was completely awake. The final change, which proved to be the most terrifying was that the general attempted to remove the covers from my head. Long bones, once human fingers, scrubbed across my forehead as the general attempted to lift the covers time and time again. I held tightly, my mind reeling in disbelief. My mouth opened to scream, but my voice was silent from horror and fear.

This was my last memory of that night. I don't know if the covers were ever removed. I haven't slept with covers over my face since then. I'd accepted the general as a part of my life, although my prayers asked God to protect my family and help us to move away. Ten years after my first encounter, God answered my prayers and enabled us to move. My visits continued until the day we left. My parents never really talked about the things that had happened, although leaving did give them courage to voice their fears. We spoke of it only once, each of us making light conversation about the horrible things we'd experienced. It has never been discussed again.

I spoke of these ghostly experiences with a priest years after we'd move away from our home in Florence. In his opinion, the general stood over me each night not to frighten me but rather because possibly before the Civil War, he may have had a daughter who was near my age when we'd move into the house. For this reason, he'd developed a protectiveness over me. There was a gentleness in his quiet vigil over me at night, although there were times when I would be paralyzed with fear. The playful way the General would pinch me or call my name sometimes during the daytime was frightening, and yet I was never afraid of being harmed.

Time and again, my family was made to endure the general's wrath. There were times, like Christmas or when Aunt Mae or my friends would sleepover, when he seemed to torment us less. This was to end, however, during the years we chose to use an aluminum holiday tree decorated with silver tinsel and metallic blue ornaments. I guess I can't much blame him for that, though. In such times, he was not as forgiving.

His presence was initially preceded by a feeling of complete stillness in the room. The silence engulfed us, giving a feeling of anxiety and unease. From the back of the house, doors would slam shut, sometimes locking, with an ear-deafening, teeth-jarring bang. The most frustrating were times when items would disappear for days, only to reappear in the exact spot where it had been originally placed. It was not uncommon to hear your name called when you were home alone, to feel your skin pinched, or feel like something was following you or blocking your path. I always felt the general's eyes upon me, even when I bathed, especially when I played.

My cousin and his family decided to move into the house when we left. I tried to warn him against it, telling him that strange things happen in the house. He laughed. Shortly after they'd moved in, I heard he'd made the comment that weird things were happening in the house. It was many years later that my parents shared their own fearful experiences, confirming at last the things my brother and I often cried about did happen. They never spoke openly of them again.

I had been able to see the general as he had appeared while alive. In reality, however, his skeletal form haunted the land I called home, his restless soul seeming to be in search of peace. Maybe that is why, after decade, no one had completed the building of the house.

Sometimes I feel I have a connection to the general despite the years and distance, which separate me from my home in Florence. I had often dreamt I was in flight and could see the lights of cities below as I flew from one realm to another. Each time I am whisked to the home of my childhood. In my dream, I walked the halls of my old home as though my soul was restless and in search of something there. Upon my return at daybreak, I felt breathless and rushed as though I had just completed a major journey.

I had often wondered if a part of my soul was planted within the walls of that old house, much the same as the general's. Perhaps the house was built over the land where he was laid to rest on his way to or coming from the Battle at Vicksburg as told by my grandfather. Maybe he did leave behind a little girl, or maybe he had unfinished business in this world, which would not allow him to cross into another spiritual realm just yet. It will never be known who the general really was. His unmarked grave had been trampled upon, and perhaps that was what tormented his restless soul.

As an adult, I returned to see the homes of my youth. My grandparent's home stands like a monument, completely covered in cob- webs now. I am saddened when I see the big country home boarded up, locked and unused, the white paint chipped and peeling. There was so much laughter and joy within its walls. Now there was only a ghostly silence.

Next door was my childhood home. I had never entered inside its walls since our move, choosing instead to view its massive decay from a distance. It appeared smaller as I looked at it from the main road. I looked at the large yard surrounding it. The magnificent pines were long gone, the axe leaving behind only a colony of rotting stumps that peeked from the hard soil where grass had grown abundantly. The black tarp stapled on the non-bricked outer walls was never covered, and years later lay faded, peeled and curled along its side. The yard, once vibrant with flowering shrubs, appeared drab and gray and lifeless. I remembered the days my mom had tended their tender blooms lovingly. I could see again my brother and I playing games of hide and seek or cowboys and Indians, racing heedlessly between each tree and shrub with our faithful pets nipping happily at our feet. Despite the horrors that tormented us, there was also joy.

Even so, I hesitated to call this place my childhood home. We were uninvited guests permitted to stay there for a short time in my life, and as unwelcomed guests, eventually we left. For years, the land and its dead seemed to scream out an injustice we were neither able to hear nor understand. It was as though the house and land had died. Today there are new homes built on the land once haunted. I pray they are instead filled with joy and laughter.

If you travel the paved roads on Monterey Road just off Highway 49, listen to the messages in the windblown pines. I'd heard the wind song as it was played to me many years ago. At last, I had found peace. I prayed the general had also.

Chapter Four

White
Purity, Reverence

Nestled within the deep, piney woods of Florence, Mississippi, Enoch's Grove Missionary Baptist Church had been a sanctuary and place of worship for four generations of Hamptons and Johnsons, my father's family.

Services were held every third Sunday, except on special occasions and during summer revivals when a picnic dinner haled the weeklong evening gatherings that filled the darkness outside with shouts of praise and spirited hymns.

The church was large inside, the pews divided into three columns with rows extended the entire length of the sanctuary. The pastors sat in regal chairs made of rich woods with high backs and velvet seats.

The choir sat directly behind the raised podium. To the pastor's right, someone banged the slow, melodic chords of "Amazing Grace" on an old studio piano. A picture of Christ was hung above her head. The loud banging on the piano caused a young baby to cry. The mom attached his mouth to her breast and continued rocking her head in praise and worship.

Situated to the left was the *Amen* corner, where a group of deacons posed stately in chairs angled to give a side view of the pulpit. This area name was mostly due to the number of times the deacons shouted "amen" during the course of a sermon. Once a deacon awakened from sleep said it three times straight, and the pastor was done speaking.

The first rows to the left of the congregation were generally where the deacons' wives sat. Sometimes they'd become moved by the Holy Spirit and begin stumping their feet, jerking, moaning, fainting, screaming, crying, and singing praises to God. It was exciting to see someone start shouting. Sometimes it triggered emotions in other people who would be overcome with tears and would begin humming softly and waving their hands as their bodies swayed from side to side.

Always nearby were ushers dressed in white dresses and gloves. Almost immediately and with practiced skill, they began to vigorously fan the shouters with paper fans made of a wide stick handle and cardboard with pictures on the front side of Martin Luther King, Jesus Christ, or People's Funeral Home.

During revival week, a visiting pastor was generally invited to preach one or more sermons. It was during one of these visits that four women began shouting.

One woman stood straight up and began to clap her hands and stump her feet while lifting her arms toward the ceiling. She began to groan, "Lawd, have mercy!" several times before fainting dead away. Three ushers carried her out of the sanctuary past whispers of understanding and concern. As they passed where I sat, I noticed she had only one shoe on. The visiting reverend narrowed his eyes at the congregation still staring at him with wide, fear-struck eyes and lowered his voice several octaves, causing a final blast of his eloquent rumblings to flow up and down the silent pews like a rolling wave.

At that moment, another woman began to rock and moan. She swung her arms wildly, knocking her hat backward and her glasses askew on her face. Her daughter and husband were taken off guard but quickly recovered and began to fan her face and wipe her forehead with a cool handkerchief.

With that, another woman began to cry and shout out, "Thank you, Jesus." People sitting behind and around her stood and began to fan her back to consciousness.

Suddenly, the melodic tune on the piano ended when the pianist slammed her hands on the keyboard. Her hat hung limply to a few curls on her shoulder as she began to sway dangerously on her seat. Within seconds, she was surrounded by choir members who assisted her outside. The pastor sang, "Thank you, Jesus" several times in his deepest baritone to a chorus of Amens and soft tinkling on the piano keyboard.

The entire congregation was moved in some way by the Holy Spirit that day. As a child, I remembered having the strangest feeling wash over me.

No one moved as several Amens and Hallelujahs were randomly shouted throughout the church. It felt good to just close your eyes, listen to the soft sounds of the summer's night, and open your heart to the word of the Lord. Needless to say, the visiting pastor was invited to return for several years following.

As if on cue, the sanctuary became filled with the enticing soft tune of "Just As I Am" as the pastor stretched his arms from the podium inviting sinners to come forth and repent. The few who straggled down the long aisleway to the front were met with much celebration, and skepticism, as their heathen ways were well known to many.

On the third Sunday of July in the seventh year of my youth, my brother and I stood before the congregation, confessing our sins and requesting approval to become baptized members of our father's church.

I remembered feeling shy, afraid, and of great importance that day. I was led to a back room of the church where my mother helped me to put on a long white robe. Beneath I only wore panties and socks.

Outside the choir sang "Jordan's River" as a crowd of onlookers—some singing, most praying—welcomed and cheered those being led to the baptismal pool. Peeking from behind lace curtains, I spotted my brother who was dressed similar to me. As he moved forward through the crowd, he appeared timid but brave.

A deaconess assisted me down a set of steps at the back of the church. I was instantly shoveled through the crowd of people. I followed those before me toward the sounds of our pastor who stood waist deep in a small concrete pool.

The sounds grew louder with each step I took. I became afraid and searched anxiously for my brother and parents. Without delay, someone placed my hands in those of the pastor who shouted, "Hallelujah!" as he beckoned me to come forward.

His hands were cold and wet when he placed them firmly on my forehead and shoulder. The water felt achingly cold as it seeped beneath my gown and rose to my chest as I stepped down into the dark pool.

The pastor said the blood of Christ would wash away all my sins, and God had prepared a place for me at his table. I tried to understand where God's house was and when I'd be invited to go there.

I looked below the fingers pressed on my forehead to better examine the still water. I wondered if Christ's blood had made it so dark and shivered in the coldness.

I had asked my daddy if fish were in the pool. He'd laughed and said I'd know if one nibbled my toes. A few leaves floated on the surface of the water. I thought snakes may be in the pool too. I took a step upward, too frightened to stand still.

At that moment, the pastor's hand clamped over my nose and mouth. As if from a distance, I heard him say, "In the name of the Father, the Son, and the Holy Spirit." I wanted to gasp for air, but he began to gently lower me toward the water. Just in time, I remembered to shut my eyes tight, and then I was completely submerged in the murky blackness.

I arose to shouts of joy. The pastor assisted me up the stairs of the pool, my hair dripping water over my face and down my back, the gown plastered to my body, my teeth chattering from the coldness. Slowly, I inched my way back to the church to change.

During the sermon that day, my family sat on the first row of the middle section of pews. The pastor prayed over all of us who had come to know Christ that day, and he invited others to come join us.

That night, I said my prayers and crawled into bed. I remembered thinking about what the pastor had said about my soul being washed by the blood of Christ, and I wondered again if Christ's blood was what made the water in the pool so dark and how it had gotten there.

I also thought about the Lord's Supper and wondered what foods awaited me at God's table. The events of the day flashed through my mind like a recorded message. My personal Bible lay opened on my dresser, the page turned to Psalm 23.

Being baptized hadn't changed the way I looked, but inside, I felt happy and unafraid. I had so many questions regarding everything. I remembered thinking I'd have to ask Jesus about it all when I visited his home in heaven. Closing my eyes, I drifted into a deep and peaceful sleep.

Chapter Five

Blue
Water, Calm

Summers at Grandma Jessie's were the best! My brother and I spent a month each year roaming the countryside with our cousin, Billy, and his sister, Vanessa, who we nicknamed "Nat" because she was small as a gnat bug.

Mornings were my favorite time of the day. Nat and I slept on comfortable raised beds in a room near the kitchen. I liked just lying there listening to the sounds of the roosters crowing and soft clucking of chickens outside the window. My grandparents, RT and Jessie, whispered to each other across the kitchen table, a pot of freshly brewed coffee between them.

This was generally the time they'd plan the events of their day. I enjoyed hearing them discuss the vegetable gardens and *Farmer's Almanac* predictions, the care of their animals, or how they expected to fill their day, even as the sun was just beginning to rise above the piney woods of Braxton, Mississippi. Neighbors driving by tooted their car horns in passing greeting. Sometimes those who lived on adjacent lands stopped by to share a cup of coffee and neighborly conversation.

Breakfast, like dinnertime, was always a big production. It was not uncommon to have cured ham, slab bacon, or smoked pork chops from the latest slaughter; grits or rice; fresh eggs scrambled, fried, boiled, or poached; hash brown potatoes; and toast or homemade biscuits.

It was generally around the breakfast table where Mike, Billy, Nat, and I planned what adventures we'd go on after the dishes were washed and the chores were done.

There was always much to do on my grandparent's farm. We took turns feeding the chickens, ducks, or goats; collecting eggs; slopping hogs, providing hay and salt for the cows, bulls, horses, and mules; cleaning barn stalls; or working in vegetable fields spread in every direction as far as the eye could see. The house was big, and inside chores could take just as long to finish.

The day had begun the same as others. Once all our chores were completed, I hurriedly dressed and met everyone at my second favorite spot—the wide swing that hung on the front porch. As the four of us swung back and forth, listening to the creak of the chain and wood, the decision hatched over the breakfast table became a workable plan.

My grandfather's lake was beautiful to see. It stretched nearly a mile and meandered past the wooded area in directions determined in many ways by the beavers that built dams here and there. The waters were peaceful and inviting, particularly in spots where sand dunes led to inlets surrounded by small patches of land.

These areas were favored by many avid fishermen who occasioned to drive past on a weekend jaunt from the city of Jackson located forty-five miles away. It was always forbidden for us to play near them. I suppose that's what prompted our unanimous foolish decision to go fishing at the lake during what could have been the final summer of my youth.

It was decided that the best way to sneak our way to the lake would be to distract Grandma Jessie. This would not be an easy task. There was very little she was not aware of as she pointed out to us on several occasions when our misbehaving ways resulted in sound scoldings.

On that particular day, we decided telling Grandma upfront that we were going fishing was the best tactic. We spoke about a small pond located in the farthest part of the southern pasture. Surrounded by small pines, it was picturesque and ideal for small fishermen. Unfortunately, the fish were too small for our lines that day.

It didn't take long for us to gather all our supplies from the storage shack behind the house. We hoed the soil beside the chicken coop and filled a can with worms. We'd gotten a metal and mesh covered can filled with crickets off the back porch when Grandma shouted from the kitchen for us to be careful and not go near the lake. We all were deliberately, shamefully evasive and said we wouldn't.

For appearances sake, we made the trek to the small pond, knowing the upward slope of the pasture could be seen clearly from the front porch of the house. Twice we looked back and thought we spotted Grandma watching us across the distance.

Once we cleared the hilltop, which slanted out to the embankment surrounding the pond, we sneaked past the hilltop and reversed our steps, cutting our way through a wooded area toward the house and lake. By veering eastward, we emerged a half a mile's distance away from the house and Grandma's watchful eye.

As we climbed over the dunes leading toward a narrow passage to a small island of land, we were joined by another cousin, Erskine, who had devised a similar fishing excursion. Erskine decided to use a boat anchored nearby. He was older, so his idea to paddle toward deeper waters did not seem illogical.

Freedom among the forbidden apparently made us even more stupid because before long, we were begging him to take us along too. Being the youngest, Nat chickened out at the last minute and stayed behind.

I was afraid some, but I wanted to follow the boys more. A small voice inside my head screamed for me to think again about it, but I shoved away any trepidation and climbed aboard. Nat watched us anxiously as the boat moved farther and farther away from the land.

About a hundred feet from land, Billy decided to play antics and rocked the boat. Water splashed into the boat all around me. I panicked, screamed, and began to beg Mike to take me back to land.

My fear spread like wildfire in the small boat. Erskine and Mike began paddling as quickly as they could, yelling for me to calm down. The faster they paddled, the more reckless they became. The more reckless they became, the more the boat rocked, and water splashed.

Within ten feet of land, I yelled for them to hurry and stood in the boat. Without thought, I walked toward Nat who was looking at me in horror from the land. Immediately, I was completely submerged underwater.

The island we had chosen to fish from was a rock bed with a straight drop to waters as deep one inch from the land as the deepest part of the lake.

Erskine and Mike tried paddling the boat nearer to me as I came up once and went down again. I remembered feeling absolutely nothing beneath me. It felt like I was suspended in air. I sputtered to the top again, hearing screams and shouting as if from far away.

Again the cold, murky water claimed me. Except this time, something solid was beneath me. As I surfaced, it felt like something solid beneath my feet was pushing me high above the water surface and then forward towards the rock bed. I took one step, falling gratefully into Nat's trembling arms.

I looked out to see Mike and Erskine struggling to get Billy in the boat too. Apparently, his bravado failed him, for shortly after I left, he stood and went overboard too. Later I was to know the horror Mike and Erskine faced having two people in the water who could not swim!

We decided to stay put on the island until our clothes had dried. Mine was the only outfit to wrinkle. The crisply pressed, pleated pink skirt set I wore was now a crumbled mess. My hair was a big frizzy cotton ball, and my skin looked like it was covered with a sheen of white powder.

Hours later, we decided to return home. With fishing gear in hand, we circled the pond beside the house where Granddad was raising catfish.

We'd gone over the excuse for why my clothes were so hopelessly wrinkled several times. With growing apprehension, we took the shortcut to the back porch and area where the fishing tackles were stored.

We were greatly blessed that day. The fears we faced changed to relief when we were all back safely together on the front porch sitting on the wide wooden swing. Except for the silence, all was the same. Nat and I kept smoothing the fabric of my skirt and top, hoping that and the humidity would flatten the wrinkles I'd learned later could not be erased with ironing.

Grandma had watched us with the hint of a smile from the screened door before asking me what happened to my clothes. Everyone fell silent as I recited the rehearsed response that I had splashed water on myself while fishing at the small pond.

Then she wanted to know if the fish had been biting. Our answers were feeble, at best. She looked at me from my muddied sandals to the top of my poufy hair, and blinked twice without saying a word, and I knew she had not been fooled. "It's too hot to be out fishing anyway," she stated to no one in particular before turning to leave.

I still remembered the events of that day. I learned that small voice inside my head warning me of danger should be taken seriously, for such it may save my life.

I also realized that something obtained through deceit is not worth the pain of being dishonest to someone you love and trust.

I didn't fish again after that day, and I never really overcame my fear of the water. If you asked me, I'd still agree with Grandma Jessie that it's just too darn hot to go fishing even on the coldest day of winter!

Chapter Six

Lavender
Grace, Elegance

One summer during my youth, Lawanda and I attended day camp at the Young Men's Christian Association (YMCA). Each day, we traveled from our home in Florence, Mississippi, to the city of Jackson, located thirty miles away.

Camp began promptly at eight o'clock every morning. Wanda and I were usually the first kids to arrive, giving plenty of time for the person dropping us off to make it to work on time.

The red brick building was erected next door to the Red Apple Café on Farish Street, the central location of other black-owned businesses including barber and beauty shops, the Paramount movie theater, Collins Funeral Home, and two Steven's Kitchens restaurants. Churches stood magnificently across the street and on neighboring corners.

The rooms were large and filled with every type of equipment including movie projectors, art supplies, and stage production materials.

A schedule was posted each day showing the activities we could participate in.

In art class, we made wallets or purses of leather and strings, hanging baskets of twine and beads, and erected buildings of Popsicle sticks.

Lunchtime was usually spent in this area. My packed lunches contained fruits, chips, and tuna or barbeque pulled pork sandwiches.

Milk and ice cream treats were provided at camp. My favorite treat for lunch was pulled pork sandwiches with chocolate milk.

Educational periods in the assembly room were spent reading, writing essays, and solving math problems.

The music rooms were equipped with instruments of every kind including my favorite, the piano. Classes were provided for those interested. In the afternoon, the hallways were filled with various melodic sounds coming from the instruction rooms. When classes were over, I'd sit at the piano and pretend I was performing on stage or playing for the choir at my church.

There were games outside as well, but they were not my best. I usually did not perform well in rough athletics, to the dismay of my teammates.

We were restricted from playing beyond a fenced side yard for our own safety. There were times when we were taken on field trips to the movies or for informative visits in the neighborhood.

A few times we were allowed to buy lunches at the Red Apple Café next door. The specialties for lunch were pigear and smoked sausage sandwiches. The café was small inside, packed full of dining tables, a jukebox, and a narrow bar surrounding the area where people worked preparing meals.

The smoked sausage sandwiches were legendary in those parts. Having sampled a nibble from another kid's lunch one day, I was determined to get one of the hero-sized meals for myself.

A loud soulful music vibrated the pavement through the propped open door of the café. The beauty salon next door was where Lillian, my mom's friend and hair stylist worked. I waved at her before stepping into the café. I became a bit nervous as several people glanced momentarily from their plates when I entered the room.

During my first visit to the Red Apple, I stood behind swivel stools at the bar and timidly ordered the infamous smoked sausage sandwich. The first bite was heavenly! The taste of spices filled my mouth and obliterated my senses while sausage oils and mayonnaise oozed from the corners of my mouth. When done, I closed my eyes in reverence for something so good.

This was not to be my last trip, however. By the end of the summer, I was walking into the café, placing my order for a sausage sandwich while rocking on a swivel stool, pick up my order, and have the meal devoured before grease from the sandwich had had a chance to stain the bag.

By the time camp had ended, I had developed another favorite snack. The office area at the Y was filled with candy and other goodies. I was well-known that summer for eating Mr. Goodbar candy bars like there was no tomorrow. I even bought one from another kid once in order to satisfy my chocolate and nut craving.

When school began in September, I had gained a whopping fifteen pounds. Fortunately, I grew an inch, which helped to hide the pounds too much good but unhealthy eating had produced.

I remember the summer when I discovered a whole new world of adventure at the Y. The times I spent there really did become a lifelong memory as the instructors had predicted.

I'd learned so much that year, developing a greater appreciation of music, reading, art, and good food. Each, I have found, must be taken in moderation for the ultimate lifelong enjoyment.

Sitting at the shiny black grand piano, I'd lost all thought of red link and BBQ sandwiches or Mr. Goodbar candy. I rubbed my fingers over the keys and imagined I was dressed in a long formal gown and competing in the Miss America pageant. I sat regally and gracefully, my head raised confidently as I performed the most difficult sonata. I was in every way an elegant and refined young lady worthy of the beautiful tiara crown.

I begged Mom for a piano that whole summer, but the most my parents could afford to give me at Christmas was a small tabletop piano with only twenty keys. I played songs on that toy until the keys were faded and broken. It was stored in my parents' attic and placed lovingly beside Chatty Cathy, Barbies, Baby Bright, Slurpie, Susan my four foot walking doll, my wedding gown and veil.

    I purchased my first piano after graduation and enjoyed teaching my children and grandchildren the joy of music. I am reminded of that summer and wonder what artistic discoveries await them.

Chapter Seven

Brown
Outdoors, Endurance

F*ollow the leader, but beware.* That taunt was one I heard often but ignored during my childhood. Follow the leader was one of many games played among the grandchildren at Grandma Ada's house.

The rules were pretty simple too. All we had to do was walk behind the leader of the group and do exactly what they did. Those who could not were removed from the line until a new leader was chosen.

This was fine except for cases when the leader was nearly ten years older than the smallest person in the lineup. Such was my situation one summer day when a friendly game of follow the leader turned into an experience similar to a day at boot camp.

Like a line of worker ants, the six of us tromped from one end of my grandparent's yard to the other—over muddy holes and in them, climbing over fences under and through them. Running fast or walking slowly, we trudged onward.

I felt confident I could remain in the game until we reached my grandfather's barn. At that point, my cousin began to shimmy up the side of the barn, and before I could guess, what he intended us to do, he jumped. The challenge to follow him was made.

Everyone ahead of me had already jumped by the time I made it to the rooftop. As I looked down, they yelled for me not to try it and go back down. It didn't appear to be *that* high, so I threw caution to the wind and jumped too.

Everyone came running when I landed with knees bent, my arms and face bruised and covered with dirt. The impact caused scratches on my knees and hands. A tooth caused a permanent scar beneath my bottom lip.

My top tooth became loosened, and my gum began to bleed. In a panic, I ran home to get help from Mom. My thoughts were already on the tooth fairy who may come to visit our home that night.

Twenty minutes later, my mouth was minus the tooth wrapped neatly in a handkerchief beneath my pillow. My grandmother had become angry when she saw me after my fall. I was anxious to show her I was okay and that I had lost a tooth. On the way to her house, I tripped, and the tooth fell out next to the gap on my gum.

I was drooling blood, so I turned back toward home on the pathway. All cleaned up, I placed it in the handkerchief and left again for Grandma Ada's. I tripped again on my way home and loosened a bottom tooth.

Ten minutes later, I placed my third tooth in the handkerchief and was about to leave again when my mom said it would probably be a good idea for me to sit still for a while. There was no telling how many teeth I would have lost otherwise.

The next morning, the handkerchief beneath my pillow was gone. In its place were three crisp one-dollar bills.

I whooped with joy and began to dance around my room. In midstride, I caught a glimpse of my smiling face in the mirror. The snaggle-toothed grin was definitely something only a mother could love.

I rolled my tongue over tender gums and then tentatively pressed my fingertip to test the strength of my remaining teeth.

Follow the leader, if you dare. Follow the leader, but beware. It was foolish of me to take such a risk jumping off the barn when my injuries could have been more severe. I made a vow to never take chances like that again, for that day anyway.

I folded the bills into small squares, stuffed them in my Cuppie Doll bank, then turned to leave the room. The sad reflection in the mirror beckoned me to hurry. It was time to brush.

Chapter Eight

Red
Passion, Desire

The summers of my childhood were happy times. Each day, from early morning until sunset, the community was filled with kids seeking fun and adventure. Forgotten were the endless days of winter when students crowded school hallways and dedicated instructors challenged each person to succeed.

There were many things to do in the summertime. When I was younger, I'd spent countless hours playing leapfrog, London Bridge, hide-and-seek, follow the leader, ball and jacks, marbles, and card games with my brother and cousins. As we grew older, we relied more on board games such as Monopoly, Operation, The Game of Life, checkers, chess, or backgammon.

My grandmother ironed clothes for a charge. She had several customers who lived off Highway 49 in Plain, Mississippi. They'd bring baskets of clothes to be ironed, some folded neatly in plastic laundry baskets. We helped my grandmother with the ironing, allowing her to rest during the hot days. Her customers sometimes would pay us to pick wild blackberries for them. It was dangerous with hidden snakes and not very profitable. Most times we'd give half to my grandmother and half to my mom in anticipation of blackberry cobbler or pie for dinner. We also picked muscadines that are like grapes but with a tougher skin, that Mama Ada would use to make wine. My favorite treats to gather from Daddy Eli's garden were peanuts, watermelons and sugar cane.

Our neighborhood in Florence was made up of many large families. Three families stand out the most in my childhood memories because the number of kids from each rivaled my own family in size, looks, and athletic skills.

The Norwood boys were all handsome and fit, always ready to challenge someone in a game or sport. The baby in the family, a pretty girl with beautiful cat eyes tannish in color, inherited her mother's charm and her brothers' love of sports. Although small in size, she became a force to be reckoned with on any courtyard.

The Anderson family consisted primarily of girls, all excelling to some degree in beauty, academics, and sports. They were a powerhouse of confidence, unity, and strength.

The Mangrum girls were remembered the most, not necessarily for their ability to hit a ball but their beauty, which attracted suitors for months after their move to Florence. The range in their ages perfectly matched those of my cousins and brother who were among the throng of besotted adolescents vying for the chance to meet them.

It didn't take long for word to spread up and down the country backroads that a game of baseball was being put together. Everyone wanted to be a part of the teams playing, even those like me who were not strong players so relegated to the outfield or catcher positions.

Within minutes, a field would be erected using bags, cardboard, rags, or even trees for bases. Some would contribute bats to the game, and others, balls. The cheering fans were generally the elderly or younger relatives of the family who owned the land being played on.

Sometimes the teams were mixed, but most often, it was a challenge to see who could play better—the boys or the girls. I enjoyed listening to the taunts and jeers each side made toward the other before the games began. The boys boasted how they'd need to be gentle to spare the girls total embarrassment by humiliating us with their superiority. It never happened.

We'd play ball for hours, our skin slick from sweat and darkening beneath the sizzling rays and scorching heat of the bright sun. And so the game would continue, sometimes until it was too dark to see, the bats were broken, or the balls were lost. Dirty, tired, and sore, we returned home exhilarated and hungry, returning the next day to do it all over again.

One summer, things began to change, though. The boys didn't seem to have that same zest for victory and seemed to be spending more and more time joking around during a game. It wasn't uncommon to see someone so deep in conversation that they'd miss the chance to run to the next base. The chance to tag another team runner out was goofed because the person with the ball was laughing so much with the person dodging the ball that the runner would get pass them to score. There were goo-goo eyes making contact all around the field, and shy giggles followed even shier smiles, which held secret messages.

The baseball teams of early summer had become one. We combined to form two teams, complete with uniforms, a club, and name. The Berry's, a neighbor and cousin on Mama's side of the family, donated their pasture for the creation of an official baseball field and community gathering spot for Fourth of July and Labor Day picnics. The challenge to play was extended to neighboring communities, and soon, we were hosting other uniformed teams to our ballpark or traveling to their towns for a game.

The games became a major event, and neighbors gathered from miles around seeming to enjoy a welcomed break to their otherwise mundane days. Refreshment areas were set up where people sold barbecue meals, cold drinks, or ice cream. A set of bleachers were erected for visitors to sit, however most chose to stand or sit in the comfort of cars parked along the sides of the field.

The field was scanned for manure patties, everyone choosing to shovel away the fresh piles or leave the drying ones be. Anyone unfortunate to run upon a Black Mocassin would high tail it out of that area almost as fast as the snake. No one seemed to mind sharing this postulate chore as reminders of past games came to mind. Never would we forget the times when rounding third for a home run, someone slipped on a patty and nearly broke his neck. Or the time the bases were loaded and the ball hit to outfield landed right smack in the middle of a fresh patty. Squeamish players carefully rolled the ball into the grass and swiped it a few times before picking it up. The serious players grabbed the ball without thought and threw it to the nearest players who knew what bile would not be flying would be stuck to their gloves.

On such a day, by the time the person in outfield decided to throw caution to the wind and grab the ball, two people had made it to home plate, and another was rounding third. The sight of that ball hitting the catcher's glove and spattering cow patty everywhere was a sight to see. The stench that trailed it from the outfield was as strong as the southwestern point of the cow's butt.

The field was alive with the sounds of disgust, teases, threats, and much laughter. The cow pasture was filled with people enjoying the simple pleasures of life—good friends, good weather, good food, and a great game and not necessarily in that order.

Soon afterward, my cousin Hal started dating a great beauty and even better athlete from the Anderson family; Bren caught the eye of a local hottie from the Norwood family; Larry won the heart of one of the Mangrum beauties; and romance bloomed for San and her six-feet tall Anderson hero. They had one thing in common. Years later, they were happily married to their summer loves.

Chapter Nine

Dark Blue
Power, Integrity

Ruffles and lace, satin and silk. Pretty bows and patent leather shoes shining bright as the sun. Flowers and crowns atop long-flowing curls. A gown, not department-store bought but stitched with love fit for a queen.

How often was such a dream one I and my childhood friends would dream about. How fortunate was I to have lived my dream not once but at least four times. How unfortunate that twice in my childhood, I was made to wonder of the importance of it all.

At McLaurin Elementary Junior Senior High School where I attended school until my eighth-grade graduation, there were all kinds of people—the smart, the athletic, the lazy, the ambitious, the poor, the slightly-better off, the popular, and the not so popular. Those really fortunate boasted of several positive attributes. Those who did not usually blamed everyone else.

As for me, well, I guess you could say I was more fortunate than some but not as lucky as others. I was smart but not the smartest; my family always struggled, but we were better off than some; I was a majorette and played trombone, but I was a wimp in gym or sports.

My greatest strength was my ambition and determination to be successful in everything I did.

My teachers were my best allies motivating me to achieve, often placing me in situations where I had to speak before the entire school assembly, sing in drama productions, dance, or compete against other classmates for honorary titles. They did the same for a handful of other students too. Whether right or wrong, we were pitted against each other in class elections, each given an equal chance to win a particular title and crown, the most popular being the ones overseeing the festivities and celebrations of springtime on the first day of May. My name was placed in the class elections for May queen four times. I won the elections each time.

Springtime is my favorite time of year, and I loved the May Day celebrations more than anything. The school was always full of fun and activities. Each class participated in some way with the festivities including dances, songs, plays, music, and always the traditional decoration of the maypole. I loved watching the many colors of crepe paper form a woven pattern on the pole as dancers looped their paper ribbons once over and once under while dancing around and around to the sound of loud, cheerful music. At home, I would be busy helping Mama prepare canned fruits, vegetables and jams that she would distribute to friends and relatives on our next visit.

How wonderful it had all been. The sounds that filled the auditorium were constant throughout the day. Arms tucked, I was escorted from one end of the building to a center stage where I and my escort were crowned king and queen for our class. I had been proud to take my place among the other honorees, dressed in formal attire, overseeing the pageantry from above on makeshift thrones.

The annual events held a secret special meaning for me also because it was my birthday. My classmates often teased me about it. I never had birthday parties growing up and only once shared a party with a cousin five years younger than me. Often I daydreamed that the entire school was celebrating my birthday with an all-school party rather than welcoming spring as it really was.

I've heard it said that a person becomes a product of his own choosing. I was chosen by my class to be its May queen a fourth and final time. Unlike one who suffers the consequence of his own actions, however, I was ridiculed by some teachers and students for actually accepting the title a fourth time. Some parents voiced concerns that I was too selfish and should be made to relinquish my title to others, most likely their own child.

I'll never forget how deeply it hurt me when my parents were told the title would be given to the runner up that year instead of me because I shouldn't be allowed to win all the time. It was an election, after all. Several visitors came to our home that night, including the Mama of the girl who would be crowned instead of me. I remembered how awkward it had been for our parents to speak, each sympathetic but wishing to spare pain of any kind to their own child. In the end, Mama placed the white satin gown she'd sewn at the back of my closet and held me while I cried a long, long time that night.

A week later, my brother and I stood outside my bedroom window where my Mama took a photo of us dressed for the May Day celebrations. Mike had won the May king title for his class and was dressed very handsomely in a black suit and tie. I stood beside him dressed in a standard uniform of red skirt and white blouse. I thought of the beautiful gown with smocked bodice and puffed sleeves hanging in my closet. Fighting the urge to cry, I lifted my chin slightly and smiled sadly at the camera.

That day, the music continued to blare over the loud speaker long after we had completed the final tying of the ribbons on the maypole. All around each class was busy with some form of activity. On the center stage, the May kings and queens all sat in regal positions, all of them resplendent in their formal wear with crowns glowing atop their heads like silver halos.

I heard the laughter of my classmates, all excited and cheerful as we stood beneath the decorated maypole. I stopped to flick a speck of dust from my shirt then touched the woven colored ribbons with pride as the school principal declared it the best ever.

I took a long look at everything around me, forming a memory, which I can recall in its exactness even today. I saw my brother sitting next to his queen. She said something to him. He nodded his head and smiled at her, and then to me. I looked at our queen, determined to swallow any resentment I felt for the one who had taken my rightful place on the stage.

Instead of anger, however, I remembered thinking how beautiful she looked, her ivory gown of ruffles and lace, her hair long and flowing, her eyes positively twinkling with happiness.

I had known such happiness not once but three times. How selfish it would have been to channel such joy for oneself only. I knew then that I had done the right thing by relinquishing my title that year.

Although being elected May queen was an honor, it was not the most important thing after all. Everyone in my class had an important role to play, no matter how small, and each person was equally important. Learning to forgive and love each other was the most challenging for us, but perhaps, it was the most rewarding of all.

Our class was given an award that day for the best decorated maypole. Our king and queen smiled proudly at us and waved their thanks to the cheering crowd.

Our queen smiled at me then, perhaps to convey her thanks. I smiled a welcome to her in return, knowing she and I would remember that day for years to come. Still smiling, I certainly hope so.

A year later, I danced onstage and was elected Junior Miss McLaurin in a landslide election by the elementary and junior high school students. My cousin, Brenda, sang, "I Believe" in a similar contest and was elected Miss McLaurin by the high school students. Some students voiced a similar demand that I be made to forfeit the prestigious title, the first of it's kind. However, with the support of my family and teachers, the school allowed me to retain the honor.

As I was escorted to the stage, I was cheered by many and jeered by some. I remembered the hurt but mostly the joy. As I proceeded through the mixed crowd, I lifted my head to see Bren watching me from the stage. Looking like an angel in her formal gown with a sparkling tiara atop her head, she smiled to me, her eyes sending a silent message of encouragement and love. Lifting my head with pride, I moved forward to join her on the stage.

Chapter Ten

Yellow
Clarity, Honor, Loyalty

The bus rides to McLaurin Junior Senior High School were the highlights of our days. Conversations were endless on topics from fashions to sports, homework to finals, what was to happen at school that day, or the events of a show on television the night before.

Many hearts were broken and romances kindled during the fifteen-mile drive from school.

More than half of the students riding my bus were related in some way to me, mostly close or distant cousins. The bus drivers were like family too. They had a rapport with the students, which invited friendly camaraderie and loyal support. The noise rarely bothered them, mostly because they were doing a lot of the talking.

There was a secret code in our family, which meant we watched out for each other anytime we were away from home and someone was in trouble. The big yellow school bus rolling through the backwoods of Florence, Mississippi, was no exception.

The first recollection I have of my brother, Mike, coming to my defense began on my first day of school when Mama had told him he must watch over and not let anything bad happen to me.

Mike had no qualms about defending me until my fourth year in school when a young classmate decided he would smash my head in every day after school.

His sister, who was four years older than Mike, tried assuring him that her brother really had a crush on me. Apparently, he had a funny way of showing it.

For weeks, he taunted and teased me, begging me to fight him back. Mike always intervened until eventually, thankfully, he transferred to another school. I often wondered what became of him.

It was not uncommon for kids to settle disputes physically on the rides home. The bus was basically divided into three sections. Small and quiet kids to front, teens and young adults to middle and very, very loud bad asses in all sizes and gender at the back of the bus. Everyone hated the dreaded invitation to meet at the back of the bus, because that meant your butt was grass that day, and someone else was the lawnmower. Some met halfway down the aisle when they were good and mad.

It was during that time that the biggest bus fight in the history of McLaurin school occurred. Unfortunately, all the members involved were from both sides of my family tree.

On the way home from school one day, a distant cousin asked Mike to scoot over to a window seat, giving up his prized aisle position. Mike refused and received a slap on his head for his reluctance to move.

He cried out, probably with some degree of exaggeration, causing more closely related kinfolk to perk up their defensive antennas for a better interpretation of what was happening.

First one, then another called out to Mike to see if he was all right. His cries continued, so they began to ask why she had hit him. Her excuse that she wanted his seat wasn't quite good enough.

By that time, her brothers got involved. Female cousins were pitted against each other. Before long, words and then fists were exchanged.

Soon afterward, it seemed that half the students on the bus were up and swinging at somebody. The driver stopped the bus and demanded that everyone sit down. Names were recorded to be turned in to Principal McLaurin's office the following day. Throughout it all, Mike never gave up his seat.

Defending family honor wasn't worth much when news reached my Grandma Ada that practically our entire family had been involved in a bus fight. She was fit to be tied when she found out the others involved were family too. She said disgrace had fallen upon all of our family that day.

Punishment had been doled out to everyone involved. Still, Grandma Ada would not be satisfied until formal apologies were both given and received. It took years for everyone to live that down. Family disagreements were forbidden, except at home.

Years later, I had begun to receive daily threats from a girl new to our school who it seems, upon our first meeting, took an instant dislike of me. We bumped heads over everything but mostly her determination to sway my schoolgirl crush. It didn't take much effort, for he turned out to be someone else's all along.

Mike graciously fought off any threats new girl or her sister issued to me, despite the fact that he and I were fighting at home, and Mike not-so-secretly had a crush on new girl.

In my seventh year, however, Mike announced at dinner that he could no longer be my personal bodyguard because I was bound to get him killed one day.

Fortunately, new girl and I never had the fight so many people felt would require ringside seats. The last time she threatened me, she dared me to meet her after school at the top of a hill half a mile's distance between our homes. Mike made me walk the long distance alone, and thankfully she was not there.

During those years in school, I developed a hatred of violence, particularly those of a domestic nature. And believe it or not, my old nemesis and I realized we had more in common than we knew and are now lifelong friends.

Even more, I was aware of the unending support of my family and their unwavering love despite any differences we were made to face among each other. Disagreements within the family unit were insignificant whenever someone was threatened or hurt.

There was much to be said about the secret code of family and friendships. It transcends time and knows no boundaries. Like a precious jewel, it is priceless and should be treasured always.

Chapter Eleven

Green and *Gold*
Renewal, Hope

The auditorium at McLaurin was by far the heartbeat of every social event in the school. Every meeting of major importance was held within its cramped walls.

The main floor where men and women basketball heroes had been born was today filled to capacity with students from grades one to twelve. The gray metal chairs they sat on were lined in equal number of rows on both sides of a painted divider line.

All lower classes were split on both sides of the room. The bleachers began twelve feet off the floor and stretched to the overhanging rafters. A row of small locked windows encircled the room. The film of dirt on them made it nearly impossible to see outside.

I sat there during a crowded basketball game watching the sky darken after the assassination of President John Kennedy was announced on a transistor radio, and the game was stopped and school was dismissed early that day. I'll always remember the dark, ominous clouds that turned daytime to night, the stillness and heaviness of the air and quietness that preceded one of the worst lightning and thunder storms I have yet to witness again in my lifetime. The angry, roiling clouds and deafening booms reminiscent of God's own wrath and shame at mankind's murderous cruelty unleashed upon the world, causing Grandma Ada's home to visibly shake as we huddled together in solemn, reverential fear while photos of Jesus and John Kennedy shifted sideways on the living room wall.

Chapel meetings were times set aside when visitors would speak on topics of health, welfare, or issues related to the community. Each classroom rotated the responsibility of providing the general assembly with prayer and entertainment from plays to song and dance.

Principal TC McLaurin was a small man, less than five feet tall, with beautiful brown skin especially on top of his balding head. He was quiet in nature but highly intelligent and respected throughout the school district and community.

He spent time at the end of each assembly with informative chatter meant to benefit everyone, but he was often disrespected by those who spent more time joking of his size or nature rather than listening to the importance of his words.

Many times those same students visited his office on less pleasant occasions. I don't suppose his size mattered much at all then. Of course, their discussions tended to follow ways of revenge after that.

On this day, however, Principal McLaurin made the very important announcement that Mr. Gray, the school's chorus and music director, had accepted a position in another district. He introduced a stumpy little man to his left as Mr. Jones, the new music director out of the city of Jackson.

"That's Jiving Jones," someone shouted on the floor, leaving everyone to wonder how he knew the club performer. A flurry of whispers followed but quickly died to a quiet when Mr. Jiving himself rose to wave at the assembly staring at him with much curiosity.

The steel guard rails that lined the brick wall leading to the floor gave a poor glimpse of a man with no face or no feet depending on whether my head was too high or low. The full view left me feeling disappointed, because Mr. Jiving was the opposite of Mr. Gray who I secretly dreamed I'd marry one day.

The bus was alive with talk of the director all the way home. Everyone was sad to hear that Mr. Gray was no longer at school but were equally excited that a real-life musician had taken his place.

Someone told Mike that Mr. Jiving played trumpet with a group called *The Velveteers*, so he'd quickly become Mike's hero. He'd spent all afternoon polishing his trumpet and practicing in front of the mirror like he was Louis Armstrong or somebody.

"I don't know why you're getting all excited anyway," I complained. Mr. Jiving looked short and dark with a big stomach and even bigger bulging eyes. *He's nothing like Mr. Gray*, I thought in more ways than one.

"Shoot, Mr. Jones is neat!" Mike praised his new hero but especially credited his being a genius to the fact that he knew how to blow a horn. "Just wait. He's gonna turn it out!"

Mike grabbed his horn and headed for the mirror again. This time, the higher notes caused him to raise his shoulders to ear level and blow until his whole body shivered.

Mike said the word was out that Mr. Jiving said he could play every instrument and perform every position in the marching band. I became fed up with talk of the man. "Don't be stupid," I shouted. "He aint *that* good!" All the same, I spent the next hour twirling my baton and practicing my high kicks.

The days that followed took some getting used to. Mr. Jiving had burst upon the scene with a vengeance, it seemed. The days of singing choruses and performing musicals were truly a thing of the past. The music room where everyone gathered at fifth period was alive with a new beat. Literally.

One of the first things Mr. Jiving declared during his first meeting with all thirty-six members of the marching band and majorettes was that it was a new day, and we'd all be marching to a different drum.

On a podium in the middle of the room, he stood tall and as straight as his protruding belly would allow him to and declared our freedom from musical ignorance from that day forth. He was on a mission of sorts, and those of us who didn't want to follow the new way of doing things could leave. Jiving Jones was in the house, and *he* wasn't going anywhere.

Classes immediately began in music history and theory. The days of homespun inherited musicality were over. Everyone who was a member of the Marching Tiger Band was required to play an instrument. As far as he was concerned that included even those who twirled and shimmied their backsides.

Gone were the days during off-seasons when the majorettes could settle into study groups during fifth period. Mr. Jiving yanked all of them back to the music room in one big swoop. A sound lecture on their failed efforts to skip band was not as cruel as his placing instruments in each of their hands and instructing them to play.

Those having to practice starting with book one, were shoved unceremoniously into a room about the size of broom closet where sheet music and instruments were stored. They were told to find an instrument they would grow to love. And they did.

After weeks of being in the tight space, I became claustrophobic and drew up enough courage to approach the strange-looking man about it.

He was in the process of conducting the more accomplished players through a measure of "I Heard It through the Grapevine" when he turned to see me approaching him cautiously holding the trombone four cousins before I had played.

I looked at the silly little man perched on a stool like a bullfrog. "It's too hot in there," I protested. "And there's barely enough room for us to sit, much less play our instruments," indicating the side on my trombone that had been dinged when I had to turn into a metal stand to keep from ramming the slide into someone's legs.

"Why don't you join us out here then," he suggested, knowing we were far from experienced players. And when I would have protested, he added sarcastically, "If it's *that* hot in there." He focused his big, bulging eyes on me and waited.

I quickly lost all my courage and felt like melting into the linoleum floor. Somewhere in the room, someone tooted softly on a trumpet like they were issuing a warning. Without looking up, I knew that was my brother telling me to zip my lip and high tail it out of there. All of a sudden, the heat in the small room was not nearly as hot as it was there at that podium.

Nearly dragging the trombone in my dash back into the room, I shut the door to the sound of the director's barely muffled chuckle.

Dismissing our plight in the tiny, hot room, he rapped his baton on the metal music stand. "Okay, let's take it from the top," he pronounced. "And a one, and a two…"

The months that followed awakened all of us to a different level of music appreciation. Fifth period became a time of discovery and new adventures.

Mr. Jiving issued tryouts for a new group to the Marching Tigers. About twenty high-steppers were placed behind the band, and so to not be confused with flag carriers or majorettes, he gave them the title of Rangerettes. A pun maybe to our Tiger mascot.

In the months that followed, he choreographed half-time routines that had the majorettes nursing grass burns on their backs, knees, and bottoms. The swaying of their hips was hypnotic, almost vulgar, and caused them to blush and giggle, Papas to stare dumbstruck and Mamas to whisper *Lawd have mercy!* in the crowds.

Years before Mama had made my majorette uniforms, even stitching the green and gold tassels to my white boots. But this year the school had purchased uniforms, and we wore them with pride. The dark green fabric with bright gold buttons and cording across the chest also with small tassels at the shoulder was striking even on the dreary night. Matching hats positioned low on our foreheads did little to shield us from the pouring rain.

The rival bands all stood back and watched whenever the Marching Tigers hit the field. The majorettes high-stepped, twirled, and danced their way all over the place. The band belted out all the latest Motown tunes like they were pouring their hearts into each note. They stomped their way like raging bulls instead of sleek tigers all over the place from left to right, bumping and grinding in a swirl of green and gold pride.

On his small podium, Mr. Jiving watched them, this swirling, green-and-gold machine of perfect unison and his creation. He whipped his director's arms back and forth with so much pride he nearly fell off his podium. The bleachers were filled with people, young and old, all bumping and rocking to the lively beat, including the visiting team and referees.

An hour later, McLaurin lost the game to the Carter High Wolves, its biggest rival from Brandon, by a score of thirty to seventeen. The small group of cheerleaders rallied everyone to a crescendo of school spirit that made everyone giddy with pride despite the crushing loss.

Throughout the crowd, predictions were voiced about the beating we'd give Carter the next time they ventured onto McLaurin land. And if anyone voiced a doubt that could never happen, then talk would quickly shift to the upcoming basketball and baseball seasons and all the star players.

It began to rain as the band lined up for the march back to the building where school instruments and uniforms would be stored.

The director stood beside the green-and-gold formation. The majorettes were in ready position, their batons raised forehead high with left hands resting on their hips and their right knees raised waist high with toes pointed downward. Everyone faced straight ahead, not even moving to wipe the droplets of rain that trickled off plumbed hats to their faces and waited for the drummers to strum the familiar marching tunes.

Mr. Jiving's eyes twinkled, and his face seemed to split from ear to ear with the biggest grin I had ever seen. "Y'all just think y'all something now, don't you!" he teased, looking proudly at the precision lineup.

Some of the older guys shouted back *damn right* making everyone laugh while the director bent over his big protruding belly in laughter. He was clearly enjoying the moment as much, if not more, than his learned students. "With some more practice, ya'll just might be aaaallll...right!" he added and chuckled at the *damn straight* remarks from the drums section.

The little man had brought much change to McLaurin. He had a style all his own, and he had been right. He'd promised to give us pride in what we did. For sure, every person marching off that field that night had a tremendous sense of pride and kinship to our school and what we had accomplished together under his tutelage.

I thought of Mr. Gray and the musical scores of Rogers & Hammerstein, of pink petticoats, parasols and bonnets, and of a cool hardwood floor kissed by black velvet curtains that stretched high into the ceilings, and my first solo singing performances. I missed the coolness of the microphone, the spinet piano badly out of tune, the darkness beyond the stage where I knew my parents would be seated, and the spotlights that temporarily blinded me if I forgot and looked directly into them. It all seemed to be another lifetime, and my body someone else's transplanted into the young girl standing still in the cool rain.

I closed my eyes and felt the same exhilaration. Once again, I was alone on that stage or standing inside a favorite grove of pines where my dreams often transformed me into an opera singer, an actress, or famous ballerina. With eyes shut and arms open, I'd danced and twirled until becoming lightheaded. A sense of freedom and excitement washed over and awakened a flood of primal emotions buried deep within me. I wondered if my ancestors had felt this same stirring in their veins.

Mr. Gray had taught us the love of music and awakened emotions that soothed the heart. But Mr. Jones had given us even more—a rhythm of music that stirred the passions of our souls. I suddenly felt embarrassed and ashamed for every negative word I had made about the man.

The director whizzed past me then, his chest pushed outward as he practically gurgled with excitement. "Mae Etta, take them on in!" he ordered, still smiling widely. The drum majorette nodded and blew her whistle long and hard, signaling the formation to attention as the drummers began the *rap-a-tap-tap* in their familiar signature beat.

I raised my right knee even higher and gripped my baton firmly within the crook of my right arm. The wind whipped the plumb on my hat, and a loose tassel string tickled the side of my neck.

With another long and then three short blows of her whistle, Mae Etta held her knee chest high through eight drum beats before facing forward to lead the procession through the cheering crowd that had gathered alongside. At last, the mighty tigers were on the prowl.

Mr. Jones winked and cheered and bounced around excitedly until he bumped into a few people who he patted with half-hearted apologies. He seemed to look directly at me as we got closer, and from that moment forward, I knew I'd never think of him the same.

What a funny little man, I thought as we pranced by in exact precision. A smile touched my lips, and I heard him giggling beside me as if he knew he'd won the battle between us. *Truly, the most beautiful person I know*, I said at last.

Chapter Twelve

Silver Tinsel Trees & Blue Ornaments

Innocence, Tranquility

When I think of my brother, Mike, I relive all of the wonderful memories of times long ago when we were young and life seemed endless.

I hold close to my heart the sound of his laughter, his gentle touch and mischievous smile, and I will have an overwhelming desire to somehow reverse time beyond that painful moment years ago.

My favorite memories are at Christmastime for I remember well the gathering of family and church and carols blasting from a stereo hi-fi, Mama Ada's cherished plant that bloomed only at Christmas, the smells of baked goodies, and Mom's green gelatin mold with walnuts and fruit cocktail.

We proudly erected the small aluminum tree in front of the large picture window, not caring that it was artificial or that the shiny blue ornaments were used year after year and had lost most of their gleam. Mike and I counted the mounting gifts that surpassed the miniature tree, both of us anxious to see who had amounted the most or the largest in size.

Mike knew I was against peeking into my own, so he'd offer to do it for me as long as I returned the favor. That should be okay, he reasoned, and naively, I'd believed him. We had the best time shaking each gift and guessing what it could possibly contain. Once I accidentally poked a finger through one of his. Mike taped a piece of ribbon over the hole and, hoping to ease my fears, promised Mom wouldn't notice. Later he asked if anything my finger may have touched seemed familiar.

We'd take turns waking the other every year. This particular year, I was to wake him, so Mike started urging me to bed at 6:00 p.m. I woke to the sounds of holiday music being played on my AM clock radio. I'd beat the 2:00 a.m. alarm by minutes. I ran barefoot down the long hallway to Mike's bedroom and, not affording him much time, whispered urgently for him to hurry up.

Beside the tree, Santa always left a large basket of hard nuts, holiday candies, large peppermint stick, and gigantic tangerines, oranges, and apples. We both agreed there'd be plenty of time later for eating as we separated gifts into stacks until all that remained were the few with Mom's or Dad's name penciled on it.

We took turns opening one gift at a time, beginning with the smallest or ones we'd gotten from friends at school. We worked our way through gloves and scarves knitted by Aunt Mildred or pj's and underwear from Aunt Mae. Suddenly Mike saw another much larger box with his name on it.

He tore through the wrapping, all the while hoping for the electric football game he'd been begging for all year. He wasn't disappointed, and before long, the house was filled with a loud humming noise as the plastic figurines he positioned in a semblance of football tackles vibrated every direction on the magnetic board except toward each other.

Mike asked me to play a few rounds, but I was all too busy feeding and burping my new Baby Bright doll. When he kept asking, I agreed to play football with him if he first played house with me.

He seemed to struggle with that proposition a while, but eventually, he relented. I remembered thinking he must have really loved that game!

It was funny watching Mike place Baby Bright in her high chair and feed her pretend applesauce and strained carrots. He carted water from the bathroom, filling her makeshift tub and patiently assisted in bathing and dressing Baby for bed. He watched me place the soft blanket over Baby's back and rock her gently to sleep. He let out a long sigh and grabbed what he could while tearing down the hallway toward his room. Within seconds, I heard the loud humming begin again and Mike's impatient shout for me to come.

I couldn't understand why the plastic uniformed men had unbendable arms and legs, but when I asked, Mike said that was the way they were supposed to be, and he didn't mind. As best he could, he strategically placed his team in tackle positions and even offered to help me place mine on the magnetic board. Of course, it was no surprise later when his men completely pushed mine off the board every game.

It was nearing sunrise, and outside the loud booming sound of cherry bombs and crackling fireworks signaled to every kid within a mile that Christmas Day had officially begun. Dad had gotten us some firecrackers, so Mike and I took turns lighting them on the stove and running as fast as we could to toss them out the back door. I nearly lost two fingers when I lit a short fuse and it exploded in my hand.

Soon the entire stretch of Monterey Road would be filled with kids and new bicycles, pogo sticks, basketballs, footballs, skates, or the soft pinging sounds of BB rifles being tested against every tree in sight followed with the occasional scream that someone was going to put someone's eye out with that thing!

We looked out to see if our cousins next door were awake. The glow from their bedroom lights was a welcoming sight. It would not be long before Mike and I were dressed and knocking on their door.

I returned to the small aluminum tree, now forlorn surrounded by the bigger mounds of wrapping paper and empty boxes. The blue ornaments seemed duller if that were possible. I touched the tinsel gingerly, filled with an overwhelming sadness that Christmas comes only once a year.

Just then, Mike came to kneel beside me. In his hand was an orange with a peppermint stick sticking out of a hole in it. He handed a similar creation to me while advising me to not let the juice drip all over the floor. The Christmas basket Santa had left was filled with more candy treats, nuts and fruits.

"This is the best Christmas ever," he said, breaking the quiet mood with several loud slurps. A stream of juice trickled down his cheek and stained the collar of his shirt. The sweet smell was very tempting.

"It sure is," I agreed. Unable to resist longer, I poked the candy further into my orange and began to drink. Unlike Mike, I didn't stop until my fruit was completely squeezed.

We sat there a long time stuffing ourselves on all we could hold, oblivious to the mess around us until our parents wished us a Merry Christmas from the doorway.

While Mom and Dad opened their gifts, we all seemed to savor the unhurried, peaceful contentment of that special morning. It was the magic of the season we felt or perhaps the peace of just being with family and sharing love.

I have fond memories of Mike and, although he is in heaven, I feel his spirit with me always, especially at Christmas. In the dark times when he is missed the most, his soft voice comforts and reassures me. I am filled with the memory of his beautiful smile, and with renewed hope, I find the courage to smile through my tears.

I think of all the loved ones we have lost, and I believe that they are all together in heaven. There is so much joy in knowing we will all be together when our Lord returns in all His glory. Each memory of them is a beat of my heart and will be cherished forever.

Chapter Thirteen

Beige
Unification, Quiet

The years of my childhood were times of struggle. The decades leading up to my high school years were full of forced integration in our schools and demands for equality and a better life.

In that respect, growing up in Florence, Mississippi, during the summer of 1969 was no different than any other place in the United States.

Although my family was not actively involved in the political wave sweeping America ignited by Martin Luther King and other courageous people like him, oftentimes I remember hearing the stirring conversations among Negro people across the South.

Many times, our churches and schools were filled with visitors representing a local chapter of the NAACP or someone with an individual interest giving informative talks and seeking monetary contributions to help further their specific causes.

I remembered hearing of whispered threats to my family and neighbors. As a child, I could not fully understand the silence or darkness filling our homes off Monterey Road or the shouts from my mother to stay down as she pressed a steady hand to my back while bullets sprayed from the open windows of speeding cars. Return gunshots rang from my family's secret hiding spaces behind trees, bushes, and homes.

The next morning, I learned the people shooting at our homes from the speeding cars were most likely a gang of rebels from neighboring communities protesting the federal laws forcing integration in our schools. I always wondered if they knew my great-grandfather's family were not Negro and some whites in Florence were our unacknowledged relatives.

Richland Junior High was located on Highway 49 South in Plain, Mississippi. We passed by the school on our trips to Jackson. The red brick building with white painted window frames had always seemed small and uninviting.

I was considered a popular student at McLaurin. I was an honor student, liked by my classmates, respected by my teachers, and a member of the band and drama club for six years.

At McLaurin, however, we received used textbooks and equipment from schools where whites attended. We ordered our own workbooks, however. I loved the smell and feel of a new book, and I hated having to use hand-me-downs, which others did not value as evidenced by the nasty boogers they left in them. I always dreamed of what it would be like to attend another school where we would not have to settle for second best.

In the fall of 1969, my dreams were fulfilled. Of all the worries and fears associated with going to a new school or to be the first integrated class at that school, I was elated to be able to see new textbooks with my name on the first user's line—no scribbles, chewing gum, or ripped pages or those hated nose boogers smeared on them.

I was placed in the ninth grade class at Richland along with a handful of students from McLaurin. The majority of my old classmates attended other schools nearer to their homes. My brother, Mike, and cousins were all assigned to Florence High School. September was to be a momentous occasion for all of us, blacks and whites alike.

The first day of school was uneventful. All the tension, which led up to that day, seemed long ago. It was as though we all knew we were a part of something much bigger and beyond our control, a necessary change, an experiment of sorts in which no one wanted to fail. We knew so many others wished it also.

The school itself was much older than it appeared from the highway, but it was well built with large classrooms, wide hallways, and high ceilings, which provided good air ventilation.

The teachers were a bit nervous. Some chose to state their expectations in harsh, exact tones the first day of school, speaking to everyone but seeming to eye the McLaurin students particularly when the conversation shifted to laziness or poor grades. At McLaurin, we were in the top percentile of our class. It was hard to take offense since it was understood we'd have to work hard to maintain our GPAs and passing grades.

Some white teachers made extra efforts to make us all feel welcomed, especially the science teacher who was one of the youngest faculty members appreciated by many for his kind wit and intelligence. A few of the teachers from McLaurin were assigned to Richland as well. One in particular who had shown me only distain before made attempts at the new school to be less hateful, perhaps because like the rest of us she appreciated familiar faces, even of those she had treated unkindly.

The white students had personalities no different than those I'd known all my life. Some girls had a habit of flinging their hair onto my desktop as though to annoy me. And it did.

It was ironic that my hair had been just as long a year earlier. They hadn't known me during my pre-Afro phase when I literally lost handfuls of hair daily to the shock and dismay of my mother. I wished many times that I had never seen that model in *Jet* magazine sporting two Afro puffs.

One day during the first week of school, I was selected to be treasurer of the Beta Club. Another black was selected to be vice president. I called my mother at work to tell her the news before rushing off to study the speech I had been asked to recite that evening.

My parents arrived home a few hours before I was scheduled to be at school. In my mother's hand was a package she said was for good luck. Inside was a gold and black dress, the same colors representing the Beta Club. I hugged Mama tightly and asked if she'd like to hear my speech. When I had finished, Mama looked at me with misty eyes and said it was beautiful.

That night when my turn had come to speak, I walked onto the stage with sweaty palms and nervous jitters. All day I'd reminded myself of my years at McLaurin full of pageants, band and theater performances, and numerous speeches before the entire school assembly at Wednesday chapel meetings. Nothing in my past could have prepared me for the looks I received that night, the few proud ones who encouraged me to do well on that historic occasion and those who stared curiously as if doubting that I could.

I looked at my parents who watched me anxiously, with heads held high and shoulders straight. Their eyes were filled with pride, their faces a picture of mixed emotions and expressions, which seemed to echo regrets for the past, concerns for the unknown, and hope for our futures.

So much of their lives had been devoted to the preservation of freedom and equality for my brother and myself. There was a new wave of justice sweeping our country and the small town of Florence, Mississippi.

Just being in that school, on that stage, on that night was something so many people had fought for and won. My parents had challenged me to be the very best I could be. I inherited the future they and my ancestors had hoped for, prayed for, and died for. I was no longer afraid.

On that momentous occasion, I accepted their challenge. And with much pride and confidence, I began.

Chapter Fourteen

Orange
Flamboyant, Creativity

April 1971

In the spring of my junior year in school, two of my friends and I were asked to sponsor an event at the state's annual arts festival, which was held at the city's Coliseum Fairgrounds in Jackson, Mississippi.

Our art teacher at Callaway High School asked us to sponsor an information booth within the children's pavilion where art of other countries was being presented. We were assigned the African continent. For weeks, we had sculpted and painted paper mache masks in various sizes to use for display.

We wanted our booth to be something that would be a big eyecatcher. Dashiki shirts were very popular during that time, so we agreed to make matching shirts from the wide selection of African-print fabrics at Hancock's.

My friend created a pattern that shortened the length and widened the sides, allowing us to convert the shirt to a mini dress. Still wanting to be unique, we became daring and shortened the top even more to a micro-mini length. We completed the costumes with clog slippers, mounds of jewelry, and Afro hairstyles. I'd lost so much hair experimenting with the perfect Afro in earlier years, so I opted to wear a wig.

The first day of the festival attracted the largest crowds. When we got there, school buses were already arriving by the dozens. We parked in reserved spaces next to the buses, which were lining up the entire length of the coliseum exhibit area.

We unloaded the trunk of the car where the display masks and art supplies were stored. It took several trips back and forth from the car to the pavilion hall.

On my final trip to the car, I leaned over to get the fragile, papier-mâché molds from the car when the wind shifted the wig forward on my head. I was faced with a dilemma.

I could either drop the molds and risk breaking them. Or I could take a chance that I could clear the trunk of the car, get the lid down, place the molds atop the trunk lid, then secure the wig with the six bobby pins I'd had the foresight to place in my purse.

I attempted to move slowly, thinking that would prolong the situation. I suppose I looked a sight standing there in my micro-mini dashiki dress, six-inch clogs on my feet, my legs spread wide, my arms supporting a tray of plaster molds, and the wig inching forward and sideways on my head. I quickly became the focus of every kid within the immediate area.

At that moment, the wind gathered strength and blew the wig forward over my right eye and ear. There was no hope after that. In a panic, I leaned my head farther to the right and attempted to hitch my shoulder upward.

The fragile load in my arms prevented much movement, and within seconds, the wig was whipped from my head and began to roll down the parking lane beside the parked school buses.

My hair had been curled tight beneath the wig. Even so, having the wig snatched from my head like that was akin to being stripped naked, particularly in front of so many onlookers.

One friend appeared at my side, saying she wanted to see what everyone was laughing at. She asked if I could use her help. I practically threw the masks at her where she stood, her shoulders rocking with the laughter she had fought to suppress.

I dashed away to chase down the wig, which was rolling down the fairway like a tumbleweed in a Western movie. The six-inch clogs made running difficult. My steps were a bit clumsy, but I managed to reach the traitorous hairpiece. I grabbed the back of my micro-mini dress and began to slowly kneel on the ground. People had come from inside the pavilion to see what was going on outside.

My hand was posed just above the wig when a gust of wind whipped it past me again. In horror, I watched as it rolled another ten feet from me. Raising myself as carefully as I had knelt before to keep from exposing myself even more, I managed to reach the wig a second time. I had passed a line of ten parked buses at that point.

Again I positioned myself over the wig and began to slowly lower myself to the ground. Securing my dress with my left hand, I stretched my right hand toward the hairpiece.

Amazingly, it moved another foot. Throwing all caution to the mischievous gale, I dived onto the wig and flashed my underwear to everyone standing south of me. All modesty gone, I got up with the speed of a sprinter, the wig balled so tightly my finger ached.

Laughing, pointing, giggling, and smiling kids taunted me on my extremely long trek back toward the car where my friends stood watching me with shy, empathetic smiles. Without a word, I walked past them into the pavilion.

The days spent at the booth were great. It was fun explaining the art tools and how they could be used to create decorative masks. We took turns preparing the wet molds and painting them once they had dried or acting as a general spokesperson to the many curious visitors.

Nearly everyone coming by our booth made a comment about the incident outside. I heard countless jokes about making sure I tie my hair down and how they couldn't wait to tell so and so when they returned home. I couldn't wait for the day to end because the crowds coming in the following days wouldn't have a clue about what had happened, and the teasing would thankfully end.

The days at the festival had been a success for each of us. Our other works had won in the awards competition. My paper mosaic of a Gibson Girl won a blue ribbon and first place, and my glass mosaic in a peacock design received a third place award. My brother's pencil sketches of various football scenes won blue ribbons and first place as well.

As we drove through the exit gates of the fairgrounds, I looked back at the empty parking lot and felt a twinge of embarrassment for my first day there.

We had wanted our presentations to be a success, a big eye catcher. Well, one thing's for sure. I had certainly gotten everyone's attention.

Epilogue

And so the Tigers were dispensed to unknown places where we were in name Chargers, Knights, Wolves, and Eagles. For each of us, time stopped beyond the period of forced integration when we were separated to unfamiliar and, in some cases, unwelcomed, places where, in our hearts, we were bound in spirit to McLaurin, the home of the Tigers. It was there we were cherished and nurtured and loved.

In our dreams, the doors were forever opened and welcomed each of us home again. Inside the small auditorium was decorated with balloons and ribbons in the school colors of green and gold and a large banner hung proudly, the roaring tiger embroidered in shiny gold threads roared with an intensity that stirred our souls. *Never forget*, it seemed to say.

In the quietness, the familiar chant echoed throughout the room. And once again, I was transported back to decades past where I was surrounded by so many I had known. So many who were gone forever, except in my heart. Before long, we were all singing

Everywhere we go
The people want to know
Who we are
And where we come from
We are the Tigers
The mighty, mighty Tigers!

THE COLORS OF MY YOUTH

Tears blurred my vision as I stepped proudly into the room now filled with laughter and the booming smiles of many familiar faces. We were again bonded as one, joined forever in our own memories and past glories. A final tribute to those with firm and steady hands who laid the educational foundations of our future successes, the place where we were encouraged to dream far beyond the set boundaries society placed upon us.

A new era of change had swept the South, conforming it into the image of a broken nation. And with it, the history, traditions, and foundation of our heritage was buried silent and lost but not forgotten. The alumni and students of McLaurin Elementary Junior Senior High School were disbanded into the unknown where our fathers and mothers guided us forward, replacing our fears and uncertainty with courage and hope of a better tomorrow.

Like ships lost in a raging sea, we sought the peacefulness of familiarity, holding tightly to all we had known. Some made it safely to shore guided by the generations before who stood quietly ushering them home safely like beacons of light. Others were lost forever, memories always but never to be seen again.

But wherever our lives had taken us, we carried the mantel of green and gold with ultimate pride. These were the most important colors of my youth.

The spirit of the tiger was planted deep within me, deep within us.

Our destinies had led some to places far from home, forever united in history and bringing pride to those once entrusted with our care.

Like the mighty tiger, we were unafraid and relentless.
We crouched low. We watched. We studied. And we learned.
With courage like so many before us, we found our voices.
And with a mighty roar, we pounced.

Jacqueline Johnson
Easter Sunday 1963

About the Author

Jacqueline Johnson Goon is a proud descendant of Florence, Mississippi, a small town in Rankin County, Mississippi, located south of Jackson, the capital city, where her family still resides. In 1985, she and her husband relocated to Washington State where they are afforded spectacular views of Lake Washington, Mount Rainier, and the Olympic and Cascade Mountain ranges. Their two daughters are married and have blessed the family with two wonderful sons and four beautiful grandchildren of which she is extremely proud. In addition to writing, she enjoys music, gardening, and, of course, any time spent with her family, church, and friends.

Other books by Jacqueline Johnson Goon:

DAYBREAK

THE COLORS OF MY YOUTH
(Note: This book was originally published by Christian Faith Publishing and is an updated and lightly re-edited version.)

THE BABY DETECTIVES CHILDREN'S BOOK SERIES
Book One: The Case of the Missing Cubby
Book Two: The Case of the Stolen Binky

THE GHOST OF BRIGHTON HALL

THE DEFIANT CHICKEN

Milton Keynes UK
Ingram Content Group UK Ltd.
UKHW052237011124
450591UK00001B/5